REPRODUCTION IS FUN

REPRODUCTION IS FUN

A BOOK OF PHOTOCOPY JOKE SHEETS

PAUL SMITH

ROUTLEDGE & KEGAN PAUL
LONDON

First published in 1986 by
Routledge & Kegan Paul Ltd
11 New Fetter Lane, London EC4P 4EE

Set in Palatino
by Columns of Reading
and printed in Great Britain by
St Edmundsbury Press Ltd,
Bury St Edmunds, Suffolk

British Library CIP Data

Smith, Paul S.
Reproduction is fun: a second book of
photocopy joke sheets.
1. English literature, 1945—Texts
I. title
828'.91409   PR6069.M52/

ISBN 0-7102-0913-4

CONTENTS

To Diana, Mark and Erol

PREFACE

Have you ever wondered where all those photocopied sheets of jokes, cartoons, letters, stories and songs come from? They are to be found all over the place, pinned on office notice boards, left in your mail tray, taped on shop cash registers and stuck up on the garage or workshop wall. Some people even carry a few around in their wallet. I recently walked into a friend's office only to find the following pointed comment had been taped on to the filing cabinet behind his desk – by whom he was not quite certain. However, to know the person involved is to appreciate the comment:

> **. . . while in this office please speak to me in a low soothing tone and do not disagree with me in any manner!**
> **Please understand that when one has reached my age and general state of disillusionment, noise and disturbance cause gastric hyper-peristalsis, hyper-secretion of hydrochloric acid and rumbus of the gastric mucosa and . . .**
> **I become a most unpleasant bastard!**

Such sheets are often generated by secretaries and typists and, while on the surface they are a great deal of fun and entertaining, many of the sheets provide the staff with an opportunity to air their views and let the people around them know just what they think of working conditions, their fellow workers, politics, religion and, of course, the boss.

Some years ago I began to collect examples of these photocopies and was initially surprised to find so many and such varied sheets in circulation. For instance, there were posters, cartoons, spoof letters and memos, stories, forms, tests, instructions, sheets of jokes and definitions. Similarly, all manner of humour and sarcastic comment was represented and no person, institution or topic was spared. Sex was well represented, as was poking fun at bureaucracy and bemoaning your lot in life. Politics received its fair share of commentary – usually directed at the major current political figures.

The British Conservative Party
have chosen the French letter as its
official emblem. The reason being,
it stahds for inflation, halts production,
gives protection to a bunch of pricks
and gives one a false sense of security
while being stuffed.

Historically one of the major methods of communication has been
the letter and it is not surprising that letters, and for that matter
office memos, have frequently been parodied in the photocopy
tradition. The following example however parodies far more than
the letter as a form of communication.

A VOICE FROM THE PAST

Apparently everyone in the University, including libraries and computing facilities, is asked more times than thought reasonable. to account for something or other. The following recently appeared in UCI Library Items, Volume VIII, No. II, November 1977. It is from Chapter IV of Learning Disability/Minimal Brain Dysfunction Syndrome, by Robert Sprague, edited by Anderson and Halcomb, and cites Iverson Riddle's citation of a letter written by the Duke of Wellington. The letter offers important insight into a recipient of one too many such requests. (DS)

Gentlemen:

Whilstmarching to Portugal to a position which commands the approach to Madrid and the French forces, my officers have been diligently complying with your requests which have been sent by H.M. ship from London to Lisbon and then by dispatch rider to our headquarters.

We have enumerated our saddles, bridles, tents and tent poles, and all manner of sundry items for which His Majesty's Government holds me accountable. I have dispatched reports on the character, wit and spleen of every officer. Each item and every farthing has been accounted for, with two regrettable exceptions for which I beg your indulgence.

Unfortunately, the sum of one shilling and ninepence remains unaccounted for in one infantry battalion's petty cash and there has been a hideous confusion as to the number of jars of rasberry jam issued to one cavalry regiment during a sandstorm in western Spain. This reprehensive carelessness may be related to the pressure of circumstances since we are at war with France, a fact which may come as a bit of a surprise to you gentlemen in Whitehall.

This brings me to my present purpose, which is to request elucidation of my instructions from His Majesty's Government, so that I may better understand why I am dragging an army over these barren plains. I construe that perforce it must be one of two alternative duties, as given below. I shall pursue either one with the best of my ability but I cannot do both:

1. To train an army of uniformed British clerks in Spain
    for the benefit of the accountant and copy-boys in
    London, or perchance,

2. To see to it that the forces of Napoleon are driven
    out of Spain.

Your most obedient servant,

Wellington

Time and time again you find with these sheets the reworking of old ideas and this is none the less true of the photocopied cartoons. *Vive la différence*, which was reproduced in the book *Still More Over Sexteen* in 1954, takes on a different meaning in 1985. Then it becomes *Oh! That explains the Difference in our Salaries* (see p. 141).

In some cases modesty on the part of typists produced situations where they sought to disguise their efforts – particularly where ribald material was concerned. One such attempt at concealment, containing three different items, came out as follows:

TO MY REPUBLICAN FRIENDS

The election is over
The results are now known
The will of the people
Has already been shown

Lets forget our differences
And show by our deeds
That we will give "Ike",
The backing he needs

We'll all get together
And let bitterness pass
I'll hug your "Elephant,"
And you "Kiss My Ass",

If in this world there were but two
And all the world was good and true
And you were sure nobody knew
Would you?

And if you dreamed of pyjamas blue
And big strong arms encircling you,
And if you woke and found it true,
Would you?

And if the world was good and bright
And I could stay with you all night,
And if I turned out the light,
Would you?

And if we lay there face to face
With nothing between us but silk and lace
And if you knew everything was safe,
Would you?

HELL   YES   And you would too.

INFORMATION FOR THE NEW-DIAL PHONE

The letters on the phone are sometimes confusing to the average person
The letter S is for South
The letter P is for Parkway
The letter O is for Operator
Now if you want South put your finger in the S Hole.
If you want Parkway put your finger in the P Hole.
If you don't get your party put your finger in the Operator's
Hole and gently move your finger back and forth until the
Operator comes - You will be able to make a Good Connection
Providing you don't go Off before the Operator Comes.

The examples in this volume, and the many thousands of others like them in circulation, are all part of a very vibrant ongoing tradition of songs, tales and so on which, like rumours, are pass on, but by using photocopied sheet instead of just word of mouth. In this way there photocopied sheets are a form of twentieth century folklore.

One thing we can say of all types of folklore, be it a superstition, song, story or photocopied sheet, is that the tradition will constantly change and never be static. Consequently when I began to collect these sheets the one thing I was not surprised to find was that there was never just *one* version of any particular sheet being passed around. Rather each joke, story, cartoon, etc. would exist in several slightly different forms – each being changed and adapted to meet the occasion, as it were. For example, at the time of the 1983 General Election the following set of verses, which had previously been adapted to relate to practically every post-war Prime Minister, resurfaced – this time it was titled *Psalm of Thatcher*.

PSALM OF THATCHER

Maggie is my shepherd, I shall not want,
She leadeth me besides still factories
She restoreth my doubts in the Conservative Party.
She guides me to the path of the unemployment for
the party's sake,
I do not fear no evil,
For thou art against me,
Thou anointest my wages with freezes
So that my expenses rise above my income,
Surely poverty and hard living will follow the
Conservative Party,
And I shall live in a rented house forever.
5,000 years ago, Moses said,
'Park thy camel, pick up thy shovel,
mount your ass and I will lead you to
the Promised Land'.
5,000 years later Jim Callaghan said,
'Lay down your shovel, sit on your ass,
Light up a woodbine, this is the Promised Land'.
Today Maggie will tax your shovel,
Sell your camel, kick your ass, and
say 'There is no Promised Land'.

I am therefore glad to be British,
Glad to be free,
But I wish I were a doggy
and Maggie was a tree.

However, such verses are not only directed at Prime Ministers, and during the miners' strike a version of the same irreverent verses was again found circulating. This time the target was the leadership of the National Union of Mineworkers.

Similarly the way in which such jokes and stories are passed around is itself never static and the methods used constantly change and evolve as the years go by. Consequently the realisation is that, as we exist in a highly literate and technological age, then our folklore will not only express beliefs and ideas about the current state of the world but also use the prevailing technology to circulate those ideas.

This approach is not something new: historically there has always existed a tendency to commit to writing or print the best tales and the like. It is not, therefore, surprising that we still adopt the most appropriate tools of the trade to do the job – nowadays the electronic typewriter and the photocopier.

The ability to type, draw and photocopy our efforts, as well as the types of humour and texts the sheets contain, owes as much to past generations as to the currently highly sophisticated technology now in use in offices. Since the invention of printing there has been a steady and persistent increase in the amount of information of all kinds which has been set down in written and printed forms. In fact up to the nineteenth century many texts, similar to those found in today's photocopy tradition, appeared in the form of cheap, single-sided, ephemeral printed broadsheets of which *Articles to be Observed by the Society of Hen-Picked Husbands* is a fine example.

The broadside printers supplied sheets to a wide market and the items they sold were inexpensive and proved reasonably popular. Around the beginning of the nineteenth century other forms of publications were becoming more easily available and affordable. Coupled with a rise in the level of literacy, the resulting thirst for more substantial and informed literature sounded the death knell for the broadside printers and they began to turn their production over to other types of work and publications. Certainly by the last quarter of the nineteenth century many such printers had run down their stock and by 1900 the broadside trade was all but defunct.

TO ALL WHOM IT MAY CONCERN.

ARTICLES

TO BE OBSERVED BY THE

SOCIETY OF HEN-PICKED HUSBANDS,

Held at the House of_____ Sign of_____

Whoever keepeth these Rules and Regulations shall be entitled to the benefit of the Box, but whosoever observeth them not shall for ever be excluded.

ARTICLE. 1.

We are resolved that the quarterly nights, shall be on the last Saturday in January, April, and July, (we choose Saturday night because less labour will be lost than on Monday), and that the yearly feast shall be in the last Saturday in October, when our wives shall officiate as members of the Committee, clerk, and stewards; and all disputes shall be put to their decision,—all the money to be deposited in their hands, and that they shall have full authority over the liquor, feast, &c.

II. Every member of this society shall regularly work from six o'clock A. M. till ten at night; and that he shall at the hours of breakfast, dinner, &c., be compelled to make the beds, fetch water, sweep the rooms, wash the pots, brush the furniture, and do every other part of a mop-squeeser's duty

III. That if at any time he feels himself unable to follow his employment, through indisposition, he shall balance the deficiency by extra labour when recovered.

IV. Resolved,—That he shall go to bed exactly at ten o'clock, and rise precisely at half-past five, in order to kindle the fire, and make everything comfortable for the reception of his beloved wife, before he commences his daily avocation.

V. Instead of the intemperance practiced by some people of resorting to an ale-house on a Saturday night, to get a pint of beer, he shall clean his own shoes, and his wife's, mop the floor, &c., take his supper and go to bed.

VI. The best tea must be purchased that can possibly be procured for money, new butter, refined sugar, cream, rum, brandy, &c., for his loving wife, while he contentidly sits down to a mess of oat-meal pottage and treacle.

VII. His wife will be allowed at any time of the day to examine the forwardness of his work? and if she find he has been idle, she may teach him his duty in that particular by the application of a horse whip, purchased by the society for that purpose.

VIII. All the money which the utmost efforts of our industry can realise, shall be at our wives' disposal; and they shall be at liberty to purchase, without our knowledge or consent, the most costly apparel which an extravagant fancy can suggest, such as a white silk gown, straw bonnet morrocco shoes, &c., and frequent all places of entertainment, play-houses, balls, asssemblies, and go a gossipping when and where they please, without a murmur from you, or you will be excluded.

IX. On a Sunday, every member shall go to church, carry his wife's prayer book, pattens, umbrella, if a fine day, take care to observe a due submissive distance while on the way. Though these matters may seem really insignificantly rediculous, yet in our opinion, they are of great importance, for the observance of them convinces, every one of their entire subjection, which is the utmost extent of our ambition.

X. If at any time you find your wife quarrelsome you must not attempt to appease her vehement ill-tempered language, though attended with blows, by retaliation, but must humbly go down on your knees, and sincerely beg and pray for pardon, even though you have committed no fault, and promise never to offend her again. This conduct will ensure you the approbation of the society, make you esteemed an honourable member, and entitle you to a reward.

XI. Contrary to the universal, or at least general habit of mankind, of indulging themselves with the luxury of tea, toast, &c., on a Sunday morning, you must still adhere to the accustomed wholesome diet of oat-meal pottage. If this regularity of fair occasions satiety or loathing, you must not even in that case be allowed to participate, with your wife at tea, or coffee, &c., but be left to the choice of HOBSON, who used to say to his customers, "this or none," consequently your choice will be pottage or nothing.

XII. A broken head or a black eye, will be considered as an almost certain symptom of your submissive conduct towards your dear spouse; and if it can be proved that you have received the same without provocation, you will be entitled to the benefit of the box.

XIII. No allowance will be made to him who is ever heard to murmur, sigh, or groan at his destiny; but on the contrary, a heavy fine, or exclusion will ensue, for such cowardly conduct.

XIV. Should any member of the hen-picked society, at any time become so great a doatard as to take the bed quilt in mistake for the carpet, or the pillow out of the bed in mistake for the child; or if, at shaving time, he cuts the bristles of the lather brush instead of the hair from his chin, for such mistakes and delinquencies he shall, as a matter of course, especially if his beloved wife wishes it, swallow with pleasure and willingness, the brush shank, and be compelled to wash all the baby's double's for the next 3 years.

XV. The highest encomium of praise, and the largest allowance shall be given to him who shall bear, with the most evident degree of composure, the words, idle, dirty, simple, foolish, blockish, roguish, and every other epithet which the vocabulary of Billingsgate can furnish, attended with the dangerous consequences of those dreadful instruments of feminine vengeance, viz: tonge, poker, fire-shovel, brush, pan-lid, dish-cloth, sauce-pan, pattens, slice, &c.; but should he show the least degree of resentment or passion, he shall be fined 2s. 6d., or should he meanly retort, by calling his loving wife doxy, slut, brute, or a certain word not very agreeable to the fair sex, or should he retaliate by returning blow for blow, he shall either forfeit 6s., or (what will certainly be a greater evil than a trifling penalty) eternal exclusion will be the inevitable consequence.

[HARKNESS, PRINTER, PRESTON.]

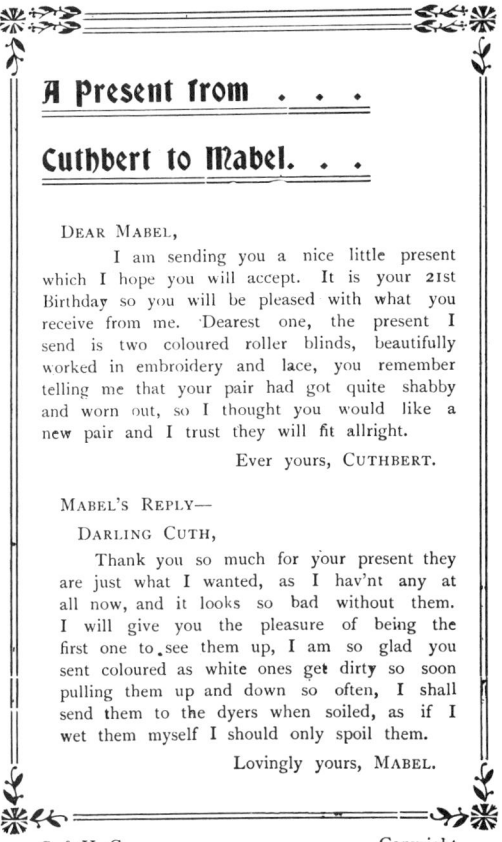

A Present from . . .

Cuthbert to Mabel. . .

DEAR MABEL,

I am sending you a nice little present which I hope you will accept. It is your 21st Birthday so you will be pleased with what you receive from me. Dearest one, the present I send is two coloured roller blinds, beautifully worked in embroidery and lace, you remember telling me that your pair had got quite shabby and worn out, so I thought you would like a new pair and I trust they will fit allright.

Ever yours, CUTHBERT.

MABEL'S REPLY—

DARLING CUTH,

Thank you so much for your present they are just what I wanted, as I hav'nt any at all now, and it looks so bad without them. I will give you the pleasure of being the first one to see them up, I am so glad you sent coloured as white ones get dirty so soon pulling them up and down so often, I shall send them to the dyers when soiled, as if I wet them myself I should only spoil them.

Lovingly yours, MABEL.

C. & H. G.   Copyright.

That is not to say that the notion of printing entertaining and humorous items in some cheap ephemeral form died with the demise of the broadside trade. Developed in the 1870s, the postcard, as an affordable and convenient form of communication, had by the turn of the century become an enormous success. It was not surprising therefore that humorous quips of the type previously reproduced on broadsides were to be produced in massive numbers to satiate the postcard-hungry market. Many of the tales and jokes found on these cards were based on double entendre as 'A Present from Cuthbert to Mabel' and 'The Village Outing' show.

THE VILLAGE OUTING.

The Parson of a Country Village was taking a number of young men and women out for a drive in a Brake. The young men being on one side and the girls on the other. When going down a little lane, Tom Jones said to a pal "Bill, it seems as if all the stones are on this side," just then one of the girls exclaimed "Oh ! Emma it seems as if all the holes are on this side," the driver overhearing the remark said "It's a funny road for I've been tossed off twice this morning myself." then the parson frowned and said "If you are going to talk like this I shall get down and block the blooming wheels.

The appeal of, and response to, this type of postcard was captured by Robert Tressell in his book, *The Ragged Trousered Philanthropists*. In the chapter 'The Undeserving Persons and the Upper and Nether Millstones', Tressel describes a story-telling session which took place amongst the painters and labourers.

While the room was in an uproar with the merriment induced by these stories, Crass rose from his seat and crossed over to where his overcoat was hanging on a nail in the wall, and took from the pocket a piece of card about eight inches by about four inches. One side of it was covered with printing, and as he returned to his seat Crass called upon the others to listen while he read it aloud. He said it was one of the best things he had ever seen: it had been given to him by a bloke at the Cricketers the other night.

Crass was not a very good reader, but he was able to read this all right because he had read it so often that he almost knew it by heart. It was entitled 'The Art of Flatulence', and it consisted of a number of rules and definitions. Shouts of laughter greeted the reading of each paragraph, and when he had ended, the piece of dirty card was handed round for the benefit of those who wished to read it for themselves. Several of the men, however, when it was offered to them, refused to take it, and with evident disgust suggested it should be put on the fire. This view did not commend itself to Crass, who, after the others had finished with it, put it back again in the pocket of his coat.

Interestingly enough it was to be the *risqué* and *double entendre* humour of these postcards which carried through to the photocopied sheets which circulate today. In fact, in some cases the two forms are so interrelated that actual texts found on Edwardian postcards are still circulating as photocopied sheets today (see 'The Misplaced Pair of Gloves', p. 114).

At about the same time the postcard was being introduced in Europe, over in Milwaukee in the USA Charles Glidden and his associates were developing a machine which was to revolutionise office procedure. The machine was the typewriter. Patented in 1868, it was to sow the seeds for the eventual explosion of photocopy-lore some eighty years later.

Prior to the invention of the typewriter the only ways ordinary people could pass on their tales, stories and jokes was either by word of mouth or by laboriously writing out individual copies of the texts. For the mass of the population broadsides and postcards were items you purchased – not things you produced. Printing such items requires complicated and expensive technology and a whole lot of skill. Such technology was, of course, not readily accessible to ordinary people. However, when the typewriter, a somewhat simpler and more affordable piece of technology, became available this was to herald a revolution in communications.

The early machines were, of course, rather primitive, certainly expensive and so initially only to be found in offices. However, their simple manner of operation provided those with access to such machines with a method of creating clean low cost readable texts. More importantly, with the use of carbon paper, typewriters allowed the generation of *multiple copies*.

It is feasible to expect that the production of jokes, verse sheets and the like was undertaken in those days in much the same way as it is now – by the *unofficial* use by the employees of the tools of their trade. Examples of some of these texts have survived from the early part of this century. One recent set of duplicated verses to come to light was produced during the First World War and entitled '*Hoch der Kaiser*'. Interestingly enough a slightly different version of this proto-photocopy sheet, entitled '*Meinzelf und Gott*', was on sale at the same time in the form of a postcard.

'HOCH der KAISER'

Der Kaiser auf der Faderland
    Un Got on high all tings gommand
'Ve Two' achdondt you understand
    'Mineself' und 'Got'

While some men sing der power divine
    Mine soldiers sing der Wacht am Rhine
Und drink der health in Rhinish Vine
    Auf 'Me' und 'Got'

Deres 'France' she svaggers all aroundt
    To much ve tinks she dont amoundt
She's ausgespielt, she's no agoundt
    Mineself' und 'Got'

She vill not dare to fite again
    But if she should I'll show her blain
Dot Elsace und in French Lorraine
    Are 'Mine' by 'Got'

Deres Gran'ma she's kein schmall beer
    Mit Bores und tings she interfere
She'll learn none owns dis mighty Sphere
    But 'Me' und 'Got'

She tinks, good Frau, some ships she's got
    Und soldiers mit a scharlet goat
'Ach' ve gould knock dem 'poof' like dot
    'Mineself' und 'Got'

In dimes of beace brepared for vars
    I vear der helm und spear of Mars
Und care nicht for ten tousand Czars
    'Mineself' und 'Got'

In short I humor every vim
    Mit aspect dark und visage grim
'Got' pulls mit me, und I mit Him
    'Mineself' und 'Got'

Meinzelf und Gott.

———◆>◆<◆———

DER Kaiser of dis Vaterlandt
  Und gott on high, all dings command;
Ve two—ach! Doan't you underschtand?
  Meinzelf—und gott.

Vile some men zing der power divine,
Mein soldiers zing "Der Wacht am Rhein"
Und drink der healt in German vine
  Of Me—und gott.

Dere's France, she svagger all aroundt,
Vor eating vrogs she vos renowndt,
To much I dink she doandt amoundt—
  Meinzelf—und gott.

She vill not dare to fight again,
Budt if she should I'll sho her blain
Dot Elsass und all French Lorraine
  Vos mein—by gott.

Und England dinks, some ships she got
Und soldiers—dey vos Tommy-rot!
Ach! I vill sendt dem all to pot,
  Meinzelf—und gott.

In dimes of peace I vork up vars,
Mein vas der helm und spear of Mars,
Vat care I vor den douzand Czars,
  Meinzelf—und gott?

Von King dere vos, und I vos Him
Mit aspecdt dark und visage grim,
Gott pulls mit Me and I mit him,
  Budt I vos first—by gott!
                    —McGregor Rose.

Gradually over the years many other items of office equipment were developed and when duplicators were first introduced, primitive as they were, they were a prime target for the unofficial copying of these traditional texts. Although the technology was somewhat different, duplicators were in a sense the forerunners of the photocopier. With the introduction in 1949 of the photocopier the potential for generating multiple copies of sheets of paper entered a new era. Initially as was to be expected, the machines were expensive and few and far between. Similarly they were primitive and produced poor copies. However, gradually the technology improved and the widespread introduction of photocopiers into offices, and the subsequent installation of coin-operated machines in public places, has meant that for the first time in history the ordinary person in the street has at his/her fingertips what is probably the most sophisticated piece of equipment created to date for reproducing multiple copies of any form of two-dimensional image.

At this point the whole thing took off: old carbon copies and duplicated versions were reset and photocopied. In some instances, particularly with the cartoons, the original scruffy sheets were just set down and copies run off. In addition, new tales, jokes and cartoons were reproduced. In fact anything that moved was photocopied – a comment which can be taken quite literally. One whole new tradition which grew up consisted of photocopying bodily parts. In its simplest form this recreation consisted of reproducing hands (see p. 14). The most bizarre form, which I have not experienced but only heard tell about, is photocopying a couple making love on the machine. Presumably it wasn't the coin-op one in their local public library. Does this give a new meaning to the title _Reproduction is Fun_?

So what for the future? As the state of the art changes and new technology is introduced it is feasible to expect that the photocopy tradition will change. After all there will be more advanced photocopiers as well as different types of equipment appearing, all of which will be prime candidates for a little _misuse_ to aid the circulation of a few stories, verses and cartoons. For example, the advent of photocopying machines that reproduce in colour has opened up a whole new area and recently examples of coloured photocopied posters have appeared (see 'No Turkeys Allowed' on the back cover).

However, it doesn't stop there. The introduction of computers into offices has meant that they are now _also_ potential condidates for

a little misuse. In fact, as far back as 1978 *The Guardian* reported on an apparent 'abuse' of the Powys County Council Computer:

IN DEMAND – RUDE RHYMES ON THE RATES

ESKIMO NELL, Deadeye Dick and Mexico Pete were alive and well, and probably in the running for a rates demand from Powys County Council. The world's dirtiest poem, all 1,500 words of it, were committed to the memory of the local government's computer bank.

But now, after an official investigation into how the lechers came to such recognition among the highly respectable chapel-going population, they have been coldly and technologically deleted in favour of Raquel Welch.

The names-dropping exercise came when it got around Powys' computer centre at Llandrindod Wells, that a 110-line print-out of 'Eskimo Nell' was available simply by asking the right people in County Hall.

The county council executive had its worst fears strengthened when rate-payers began telephoning and writing in asking for copies of the poem. 'We had to tell them that this is not possible,' said a spokesman yesterday.

Mr Islwyn David, deputy chief executive at Powys County Hall, said: 'The allegations have been investigated and have been found to be correct.' Two men have been disciplined.

Said Mr David: 'Eskimo Nell' was obscene, but the pictures of Raquel Welch were computer demonstration pieces. They are not obscene and are being allowed to remain on the computer.'

The Guardian (Nov. 21 1978)

Of course, this sort of thing is not new. People have been putting such things into computers for years and, for that matter, they still are. In Columbus, Ohio last year a student presented me with a copy of a computer printout of traditional jokes, limericks, quotations and so on. Each time someone used the computer the machine greeted them with one of these items selected at random. Again many of the verses appear to have been originally drawn from this corpus of traditional photocopy sheets.

But it doesn't stop there. In November 1984 I was interviewed by Tommy Vance on a programme being sent out by the British Forces Broadcasting Services to our military forces world-wide. The topic was traditional photocopied sheets. Tommy remembered having seen some similar verses when visiting troops stationed in the Falklands. Following up the chance to examine a few more examples, we made an appeal and some time later a whole collection of items duly arrived. Enthusiastically I opened the parcel. Several of the verses, stories and jokes were new but many were the same as the photocopied sheets I have already collected. Here were 'The Twin Brothers' (p. 118), 'London's Nine Newspapers' (p. 93) and 'Psychological Studies of Types of Men you Meet in Public Toilets' (p. 93).

Perhaps more interesting, these texts were not photocopies. Instead they had been sent from England to the Falklands on military communications teleprinter links. The same types of stories, the same misuse of equipment, the same results – use the best technology currently available to spread a little laughter around the world.

Where will it end? I sometimes have this vision of communications computers in future centuries beaming the latest Martian jokes down to Earth from just beyond Jupiter. Impossible? Who can tell?

This tradition of photocopying and circulating sheets is not restricted solely to Britain – or for that matter the English-speaking world. Instead it is international by nature and examples are to be found in any part of the world where photocopiers have been introduced – and where haven't they been? The majority of items in this selection are examples which were found circulating in Britain over the past few years. However, this is not to say that they are all British by origin or nature and I am sure that several have been introduced from other parts of the world. For example, it is not unusual to find items, obviously derived from North America, circulating in the UK. These sheets are immediately identifiable by their use of English, American spellings and so on. In spite of this they are not viewed as alien to our culture and are quite readily passed around.

In preparing this volume I have not rewritten the sheets but rather reproduced them warts and all. The only concession made was to supply the odd missing word or correct any totally misleading spelling. Similarly to have edited the text would have been wrong, for irrespective of the state of the English used, they all exhibit a certain raw immediate vitality, a vitality which is the cornerstone of this tradition. To that end it would not be appropriate for a mere mortal such as me to rewrite the visionary wisdom of these great, if anonymous, authors.

Well, now when one of these sheets appears on your desk or on

the office wall you will now know what to do. Reach for the photocopier, push the button and pass on the word – *Reproduction is Fun!!*

Paul Smith
West Stockwith

So far I have been fortunate enough to find copies of several thousand photocopied joke sheets, cartoons and posters. However, I am sure this is only just the tip of a vast iceberg. If you do come across any sheet not in this book please, please, please photocopy one for me and send it on. You never know, I may be able to include it in the next volume.

Paul Smith
c/o Routledge and Kegan Paul plc
11 New Fetter Lane
London EC4P 4EE

ACKNOWLEDGEMENTS

My foremost acknowledgement must be to the thousands of ordinary people who, over the years, have taken time out to create, copy and pass on to others, photocopies of these sheets. Without them our lives would be so boring.

The individual items in this volume have been selected from a collection of sheets I have been gathering over the past fifteen years. To that end I owe an enormous debt to Mac E. Barrick, Ervin Beck, Georgina Boyes, Derek Froome, Mark Glazer, Joe Goodwin, Cathy Preston and Mike Preston – all who made available to me their own collections. I am also indebted to the many friends and colleagues who bothered to remember that I collect odd curiosities and passed on copies to me when they came their way. In particular my thanks go to Dan Barnes, Gillian Bennett, Rolf Brednick, Kathy Dickinson, Ian Duff, Sylvia Duff, Alan Griffiths, Dave Harker, Peter Hartnell, Tim Healey, Carl Hemmeler, J. Hillyard, Jackie Hull, John Lake, Chris Lourens, Brian MacArthur, Brian McConnell, Gordon McCulloch, Donna McDonald, Peter Millington, Neil Philip, Mark Phillip, Bill Quinton, Ruth Richardson, Steve Roud, Doc Rowe, Graham Shorrocks, Ann Skiller, Tommy Vance and C. Wright.

Finally I must record the invaluable help I received from the good people who helped me prepare this volume – Mike and Cathy Preston for thinking up the title, and Helen Hartnell and Derek Froome for coming to my rescue with practical help. I thank you all.

THE CYNICAL SECRETARY

PERMANENT WRINKLES
FROM CONSTANT SMILE
AND DEADLINE PRESSURE

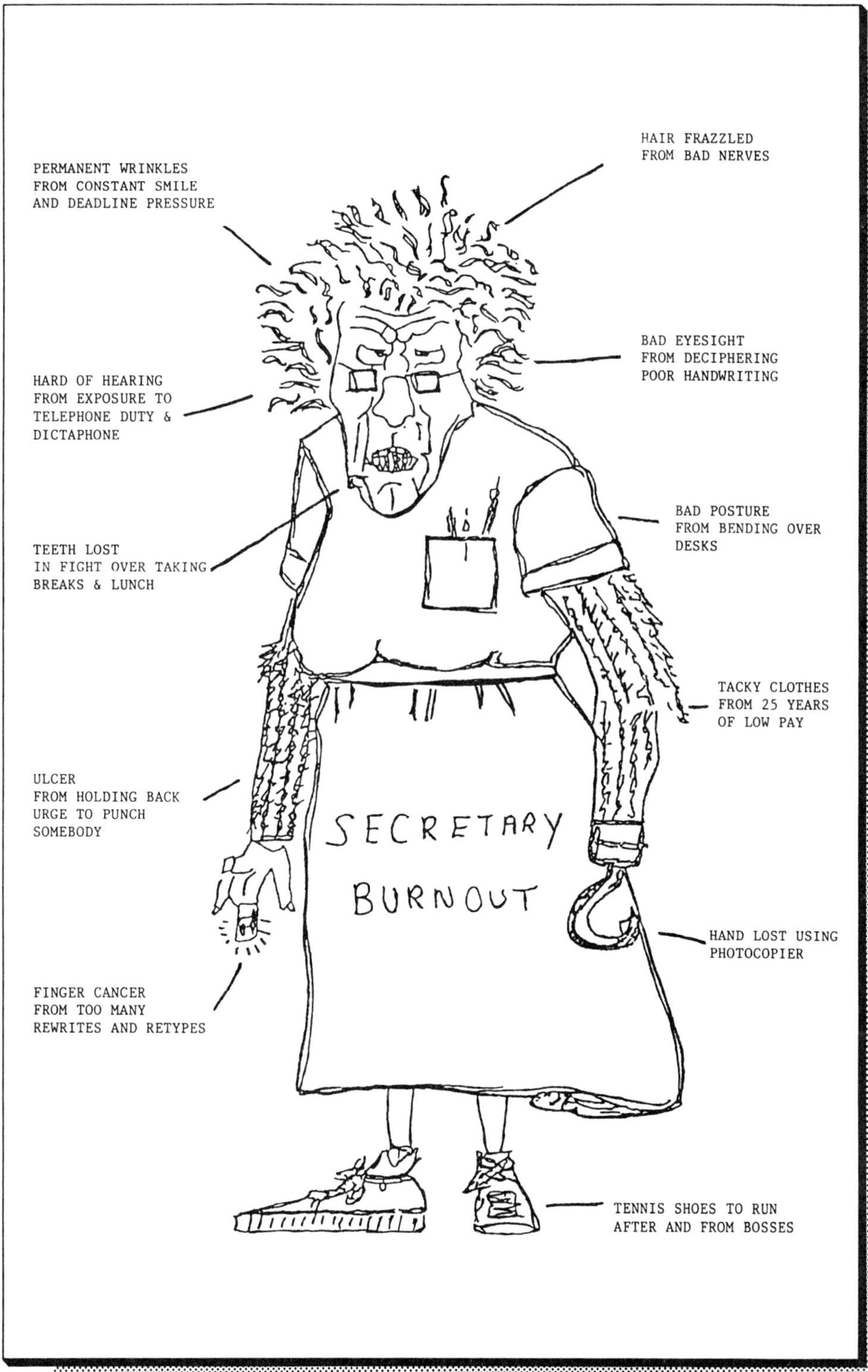

HAIR FRAZZLED
FROM BAD NERVES

HARD OF HEARING
FROM EXPOSURE TO
TELEPHONE DUTY &
DICTAPHONE

BAD EYESIGHT
FROM DECIPHERING
POOR HANDWRITING

BAD POSTURE
FROM BENDING OVER
DESKS

TEETH LOST
IN FIGHT OVER TAKING
BREAKS & LUNCH

TACKY CLOTHES
FROM 25 YEARS
OF LOW PAY

ULCER
FROM HOLDING BACK
URGE TO PUNCH
SOMEBODY

SECRETARY

BURNOUT

HAND LOST USING
PHOTOCOPIER

FINGER CANCER
FROM TOO MANY
REWRITES AND RETYPES

TENNIS SHOES TO RUN
AFTER AND FROM BOSSES

MY BOSS & I

When I take a long time —
I am slow.
When my boss takes a long time
He is thorough.
When I don't do it —
I am lazy.
When my boss doesn't do it
He is too busy.
When I do something without being told —
I am trying to be smart.
When my boss does the same —
that is initiative.
When I please my boss —
I'm apple-polishing.
When my boss pleases his boss —
He's co-operating.
When I do good, my boss never remembers.
When I do wrong, he never forgets.

MY JOB

It's not my place to run the train
the whistle I can't blow
It's not my place to say how far
the train's allowed to go

It's not my place to shoot off steam
nor even clang the bell
But let the damn thing jump the track
and see who catches hell!

"can you type?"
"no!"
"can you file?"
"no!"
"can you take shorthand?"
"no!"
"how about simple bookkeeping?"
"no!"
"what on earth can you do?"
"everything you can!"

THE BOSS	EVERYBODY ELSE
takes calculated risks	drops bollocks
is firm	is bloody-minded
takes clear positions	has opinions
knows the angles	'operates'
is straight	is incredibly rude
gives leadership	is autocratic
sets an example	affects moral superiority
tells the truth	makes trouble
goes on to higher things	is ambitious
is clever	is smart-arsed
is tactful	greases
deals with important people	licks arses
has key contacts	collects 'phone numbers
is unavoidably detained	fucks people about
has charisma	is an arrogant bastard
offers suggestions	lays down a hard line
represents everyone's interests	speaks for themselves
has natural abilities	needs to be trained
has priorities	wants their own way
negotiates	boxes people up
is self-confident	is cocky
is modest	is hiding something
enforces discipline	is vindictive
is above politics	is a tired old hack
develops the work	builds an empire
has style	is an ego-maniac
administers efficiently	is a bureaucrat
selects from the truth	tells lies
has your number	holds grudges
is diplomatic	manipulates people
tells home truths	winds people up
works people in	operates the Old Pals' Act
has principles	is bigoted
trusts personal friends	factionalises
deserves loyalty	is a glory-seeker
takes a stand	is after the top job
is sensitive	is weak
drives fast cars	is macho
lobbies properly	is divisive
knows people's abilities	creates hierarchies
is fly	is devious
gets a just reward	sells out
works very hard	does what they get paid for
takes control	exercises power
hasn't time for shit-work	is being carried
believes in democracy	is an agitator
is always in the office	hangs about the 'phone all day
does research	opens a few books
is irreplaceable	controls information
takes responsibility	believes in privatisation
is easily hurt	is soft
has the occasional fault	is a wanker
likes nice people	isn't hard enough
exercises discretion	cuts corners
utters cries for help	whines
merits unswerving faith	needs massive support all the time
does what has to be done	is an anarchist
is supportive	patronises
makes the odd error	always takes the wrong position
has no contradictions	

THE TYPIST'S TEN COMMANDMENTS

1. A typist must remember at all times that she is absolutely stupid.

2. A typist must remember that she must obey no matter what happens.

3. A typist must realise that, although her boss has never typed he can do her job in half the time and twice as accurately.

4. A typist must understand that 'typist' is just another word for doormat, tea pourer, post-mistress, mechanic, general buyer, organised convenor, walking encyclopaedia, listening post, servant and shop hand.

5. A typist must have available at all times - crystal ball, aspirins, nail file, cork screw, tact and charm, endless sympathy and limitless patience.

6. A typist must remember in times of flap and stress, that she has never worked as hard as a man.

7. A typist must remember to be pleasant from Monday morning until Friday tea-time.

8. A typist must be able to read shorthand, longhand, script, scrawl, reports, and letters written under water, in bed, in the bath, in the train or plane; written in pencil, charcoal, biro, over-inked crow bar, and also writing done under a microscope. She must be able to unravel her Master's Voice from a series of extraneous noises on a dictaphone and distinguish a hiccup from a comma.

9. A typist must be neat and tidy (and if possible, glamorous - despite the fact that she must be the lowest paid member of staff) at all times, but never, never comb her hair, make up or clean her nails in office hours.

10. A typist must remember that men are - His Majesty, Mohammed, Chief Whip, Genius, Lord, and Master; handsome, irresistable, and not that 'b.......d'. They all look like Clint Eastwood, have the love life of Don Juan, are as funny as Freddie Starr, and of course must be worshipped, respected, idolised; to be wrapped in cotton wool; defended against all comers, and loved - no matter who they are or WHAT THEY LOOK LIKE.

TEN COMMANDMENTS OF A TYPIST

1. Thou shalt not be an ornamental stenographer.

2. Thou shalt be merry; for, verily, an office should be delivered from a maid with a grouch.

3. Thou shalt not forget that the best advertisement is neat, correct and speedy work.

4. Thou shalt have the moral courage to decline invitations to dinner parties and the theatre.

5. Thou shalt not permit a dictator who mumbles his words to go unchallenged; for, verily, thou shalt not be afraid to ask him to repeat.

6. Thou shalt not mistake courtesy for a deeper interest, for in many offices there is a tendency to make the former so extreme that a tender-hearted maid might be tempted to believe it the latter.

7. Thou shalt not cherish any illusions (nor delusions) about the man who weighs your personality against the spending money for his family; for, verily, no man is a hero to his stenographer.

8. Thou shalt not deceive thyself with the false impression that thou art wiser than the boss; neither shalt thou essay to improve the language of his dictation.

9. Thou shalt not fail to proclaim an efficacious method (shouldst thou hit upon one) for getting rid of office bores - the kind that expect to be entertained while waiting for their next business appointment.

10. Thou shalt not adorn thyself with fine clothes, or beautify thy face with cosmetics for the purpose of tempting men to invite thee forth to social swirls; for, verily, thou shalt not think more of thy dress than of thy address.

THE SECRETARY's PLEA:

Give me the memory of an elephant. Let
me be able to answer four telephones at
the same time, and type a letter that
'must go today' - even though it won't
get signed until tomorrow.
Help me be patient when I search the
files for a paper sitting on the boss's
desk.
Help me understand all unexplained
instructions. Let me always know
where the boss is, what he is doing
and when he'll be back.
And, when the year ends, grant me the
foresight not to destroy - when I am
told to - records that will soon be
wanted.
Please help me accomplish all these
things and make me too good to be
true.

WHEN GOD MADE MAN, AND THERE WAS ONLY ONE, VARIOUS PARTS OF THE BODY ARGUED ABOUT WHO WOULD BE BOSS.

THE <u>HANDS</u> SAID THEY SHOULD BE BOSS BECAUSE THEY DID ALL THE WORK.

THE <u>FEET</u> SAID THEY SHOULD BE BOSS BECAUSE THEY TOOK MAN WHERE HE COULD WORK AND GET FOOD.

THE <u>HEART</u> THOUGHT IT SHOULD BE BOSS BECAUSE IT PUMPED BLOOD THAT ALLOWED THE FOOD TO BE DIGESTED BY THE STOMACH AND THEN REACH THE BODY.

THE <u>BRAIN</u> SAID 'NO'. 'I HAVE TO SEND ALL THE SIGNALS TO GET EACH OF YOU TO DO YOUR JOB; THEREFORE I'M THE BOSS.'

THE ASSHOLE SAID 'I'LL SHOW YOU WHO IS BOSS'. SO HE CLOGGED UP AND WOULDN'T LET ANYTHING PASS. AFTER A FEW DAYS, THE STOMACH ACHED, THE HANDS WERE PRACTICALLY HELPLESS, THE FEET COULD NOT CARRY THE BODY, THE HEART WAS ABOUT TO STOP PUMPING BLOOD, AND THE BRAIN SIGNALS WERE BEING IGNORED. TO ALL THIS, THERE IS A MORAL.

YOU DON'T HAVE TO BE A BRAIN TO BE A BOSS - JUST AN ASSHOLE.

NOBODY IS PERFECT

EACH ONE OF US IS A MIXTURE OF GOOD QUALITIES AND SOME PERHAPS NOT-SO-GOOD QUALITIES. IN CONSIDERING OUR FELLOW MAN WE SHOULD REMEMBER HIS GOOD QUALITIES AND REALIZE THAT HIS FAULTS ONLY PROVE THAT HE IS, AFTER ALL, A HUMAN BEING. WE SHOULD REFRAIN FROM MAKING HARSH JUDGMENT OF A PERSON JUST BECAUSE HE HAPPENS TO BE A DIRTY ROTTEN, NO-GOOD SON-OF-A-BITCH!

OFFICE
PHILOSOPHY

THIS IS YOUR RIGHT

It has come to the attention of the Safety Committee that many union members are not claiming their full entitlement under the law.

A wide variety of disablement aids and services are available for which many members could qualify with a little more effort.

> False Limbs
>
> Walking Sticks/Crutches
>
> Wheelchairs
>
> Glass Eyes
>
> White Sticks
>
> Guide Dogs

In addition to these aids a limited number of vacancies are available each year at

> Henshaws Institute for the Blind
> Stoke Mandeville Hospital

How Can I Qualify?

Strict criteria for qualification must be met, but in practice are simple to achieve. The following guidelines should ensure that all members qualify for maximum benefits.

1) Ignore all Health and Safety Rules

2) Millers, Grinders, etc., must not wear Safety goggles/Glasses

3) All dangerous machinery must be operated without guards

4) All dangerous chemicals to be used without safety masks or extractor fans

What's In It For Me?

For some years the perks available to Management have caused ill-feeling on the shop floor. The action outlined above should go some way to redress the balance.

Members who at present have claimed none of the above perks are reminded that an increase in demand for facilities and services could result in an increase in the labour force in these areas thus helping to improve the present unemployment situation.

Rules of the Game

1. Never assume anything.
2. Question everything.
3. Nothing is simple black and white.
4. Never answer a hypothetical question always suspect a real situation and probe for facts.
5. Always abide by procedural rules.
6. Never give way to blackmail or threat.
7. If possible, know the answers before asking the questions.
8. If you are wrong, admit it.
9. Know what and where to question.
10. Never panic; few situations are so serious that they cant wait for thought.

In the words of the
OLD PHILOSOPHER...

when things go wrong,
as they sometimes will,
when the road you're
trudging seems all up-
hill, when the funds are
low, and the debts are
high, and you want to
smile, but you have to cry,
when care is pressing you
down a bit....

Don't complain to me,

I DON'T GIVE a SHIT!

ECONOMY OF MIND

Thinking gives a lot of pain

Talking doesn't cost a thing,

Therefore, rest your weary brain

and

Give your tongue a fling

TOMORROW
WE'VE GOT TO GET
ORGANIZED

TABLE OF EXCUSES

To save everyone's time, give your excuse by number!

1. *That's the way we've always done it.*
2. *I didn't know you were in a hurry for it.*
3. *That's not in my department.*
4. *No one told me to go ahead.*
5. *I'm waiting for an O.K.*
6. *How did I know this was different?*
7. *That's his job — not mine!*
8. *Wait till the boss comes back and ask him.*
9. *I forgot.*
10. *I didn't think it was very important.*
11. *I'm so busy I just can't get around to it!*
12. *I thought I told you.*
13. *I wasn't hired to do that!*

THE POWER OF POSITIVE PESSIMISM
BY HOWARD KANDEL

NEVER PUT OFF TILL TOMORROW WHAT YOU CAN AVOID ALL
TOGETHER

HE WHO PUTS HIS NOSE TO THE GRINDSTONE IS A
BLOODY FOOL

I DISAGREE WITH WHAT YOU SAY BUT I WILL DEFEND TO
THE DEATH YOUR RIGHT TO TELL SUCH LIES

CHASTE MAKES WASTE

THE DEVIL FINDS WORK FOR IDLE GLANDS

HE WHO ALWAYS FINDS FAULT WITH HIS FRIENDS HAS
FAULTY FRIENDS

A FRIEND IN NEED IS A PEST INDEED

THE PEN IS MIGHTIER THAN THE PENCIL

GENIUS IS TEN PERCENT INSPIRATION AND FIFTY PERCENT
CAPITAL GAINS

HE WHO TRAINS HIS TONGUE TO QUOTE THE LEARNED
SAGES WILL BE KNOWN FAR AND WIDE AS A SMART-ASS

ALL THE WORLD LOVES A FOUR LETTER WORD

TWO'S COMPANY, THREE'S AN ORGY

A PENNY SAVED IS RIDICULOUS

ITS NOT THE MONEY, ITS THE PRINCIPAL AND THE
INTEREST

TWO CAN LIVE AS CHEAPLY AS ONE ... FOR HALF AS LONG

A SMART MAN KNOWS ON WHICH SIDE HIS BROAD IS BETTER

HE WHO USES BAD LANGUAGE IS AN IGNORANT SCHMUCK

CHILDREN SHOULD BE OBSCENE AND NOT HEARD

ASK NOT FOR WHOM THE BELL TOLLS AND YOU WILL PAY
ONLY THE STATION TO STATION RATE

LOVE THY NEIGHBOR, BUT MAKE SURE HER HUSBAND IS
AWAY

WHERE THERE'S A WILL, THERE'S AN INHERITANCE TAX

MONEY IS THE ROOT OF ALL EVIL AND A MAN NEEDS ROOTS

BENEATH A ROUGH EXTERIOR OFTEN BEATS A HARLOT OF
GOLD

HE WHO IS FLOGGED BY FATE AND LAUGHS THE LOUDER
IS A MASOCHIST

ALWAYS BE SINCERE, EVEN WHEN YOU DON'T MEAN IT

SQUAW WHO SPEAKS WITH FORKED TONGUE CAN TEACH
YOUNG BRAVE MANY NEW TRICKS

HAPPINESS CAN'T BUY MONEY

HE WHO LAUGHS LAST DOESN'T GET THE JOKE

ANNUAL 'FLU LEAVE

IT HAS BEEN EVIDENT OF LATE THAT SOME PERSONNEL HAVE NOT BEEN TAKING THEIR ANNUAL ENTITLEMENT.
TO CORRECT THIS DEPLORABLE STATE OF AFFAIRS THE FOLLOWING MUST BE ADHERED TO:–

1. TWO GOOD SNEEZES IN A CROWDED SMOKE FILLED OFFICE IS SUFFICIENT FOR ONE WEEK OFF.

2. A HACKING COUGH, BROUGHT ON BY SOME 'FRESH AIR FIEND' OPENING A WINDOW IS ALSO GOOD FOR A WEEK OFF.

3. A LOUSY FEELING, EYES WATERING, LEGS FEELING LIKE JELLY, ARE GOOD SIGNS FOR A FORTNIGHT OFF.

THINGS TO AVOID

4. EXERCISE, GOOD APPETITE, A SENSE OF BONHOMIE, FRESH AIR MUST BE AVOIDED LIKE THE PLAGUE. OF COURSE IF YOU HAVE THE PLAGUE THAT'S WORTH A MONTH OFF.

5. ASPIRIN, CODEINE TABLETS ETC., ARE ONLY TO BE TAKEN IN EXTREME CASES LIKE INDUSTRIAL FATIGUE!

6. LOOKING FORWARD TO THE WEEKEND, HOLIDAYS, OR PROMOTION AND THE SUCHLIKE CAN ONLY TEND TO MAKE YOU CHEERFUL AND DELAY YOUR ENTITLEMENT.

TAKE YOUR EASE
WITH A SNEEZE,
YOU'LL SOON BE OFF
WITH A COUGH.

SIGNED: A.V. IRUS M.D.
STOKE, COVENTRY
JAN 1978

The Pay Rise By A Good Boss

A man asked his boss for a rise in salary. The boss said, 'What do you mean? Give you a rise? You don't work here at all. Listen there are 365 days in the year - 366 this year because it's a leap year. The working day is 8 hours - that's one third of a day, so over the year that's 122 days. The office is shut on Sundays so that's 52 off, making 70 days. Then you have two weeks holiday - take off 14 days which leaves 56. There are four Bank Holidays which leaves 52. Then the office is closed on Saturdays, isn't it? Well, there are 52 Saturdays in the year - so you don't do anything here at all. Yet you're asking me for a rise.

You just can't beat a staff with

ENTHUSIASM

WHEREVER   WHOEVER   WHATEVER

To: ALL ENFORCEMENT STAFF

Reply to:

Tel. Ext:

Tel. Ext:

Ref:

Ref:

Date:

Date:

Subject: TRAINING — DEALING WITH AWKWARD CONSUMERS

(1) ATTEMPT CONCILIATION,

(2) TRY AGAIN IF SPURNED.

(3) MAKE YOUR POINT.

(4) POLITELY WITHDRAW.

COMMANDMENTS OF COMMON SENSE

IF YOU OPEN IT, CLOSE IT.

IF YOU TURN IT ON, TURN IT OFF.

IF YOU UNLOCK IT, LOCK IT.

IF YOU BREAK IT, REPAIR IT.

IF YOU CAN'T FIX IT, REPORT IT TO SOMEONE WHO CAN.

IF YOU BORROW IT, RETURN IT PROMPTLY.

IF YOU USE IT, DON'T ABUSE IT.

IF YOU MAKE A MESS, CLEAN IT UP.

IF YOU MOVE IT, PUT IT BACK.

IF IT BELONGS TO SOMEONE ELSE AND YOU WANT TO USE IT, GET PERMISSION BEFORE TAKING IT.

IF YOU DON'T KNOW HOW TO OPERATE IT, LEAVE IT ALONE!

```
                    ! WARNING !
          THIS MACHINE SUBJECT TO BREAKDOWNS
          DURING PERIODS OF CRITICAL NEED!!!
```

A SPECIAL CIRCUIT IN THIS MACHINE CALLED A "CRISIS DETECTOR" SENSES THE USER'S EMOTIONAL STATE IN TERMS OF HOW DESPERATELY HE OR SHE NEEDS TO USE THE MACHINE. THE CRISIS DETECTOR THEN CREATES A MALFUNCTION PROPORTIONAL TO THE DESPERATION OF THE USER. THREATENING THE MACHINE WITH VIOLENCE OR THE USE OF CURSES AND OBSCENITIES MAY SOOTHE THE USER BUT WILL NOT FOOL THE CRISIS DETECTOR AND WILL ONLY AGGRAVATE THE SITUATION. LIKEWISE, ATTEMPTS TO USE ANOTHER MACHINE MAY CAUSE IT TO MALFUNCTION, BECAUSE THEY BOTH BELONG TO THE SAME UNION. KEEP COOL AND SAY NICE THINGS TO THE MACHINE. NOTHING ELSE SEEMS TO WORK . . .

DR. JAMES NORTON, IUPUI

BUREAUCRACY AT ITS BEST

MEMORANDUM

TO: ALL MANAGERS

FROM: CHRISTMAS CHAIRMAN

SUBJECT: DECORATING OFFICE FOR CHRISTMAS

DATE: DECEMBER 4, 1968

We have been informed by Washington that a White Christmas would be in violation of Title II of the Civil Rights Act of 1964. Therefore, the following steps are to be taken in order to insure that we comply with the Act during the Christmas season in our offices:

1. All Christmas trees must have a least 23.1% colored bulbs and they must be placed throughout the tree and not segregated in the back of the tree.

2. Christmas presents cannot be wrapped in white paper. However, interim approval can be given if colored ribbon is used to tie them.

3. If a manger scene is used, 20% of the angels and one out of the Three Kings must be of a minority race.

4. If Christmas music is played, "We Shall Overcome" must be given equal time. Under no circumstances is "I'm Dreaming of a White Christmas" to be played.

5. Care should be taken in party planning. For example:

    a. Use pink champagne instead of white.
    b. Turkey may be served but only if the white and dark meat are on the same platter. There will be no 'separate but equal' platters permitted.
    c. Use chocolate royale ice cream instead of vanilla.
    d. Both chocolate and white milk must be served. There will be no freedom of choice plan. Milk will be served without regard to color.

A team from Washington will visit us on December 25th to determine our compliance with the Act. If it snows on Christmas Eve, we are all in trouble.

NOTICE

It has come to the attention of the Management that employees have been dying on the job, and either refusing, or neglecting to fall over. This practice must cease forthwith; any employee being found dead on the job in an upright position will immediately be dropped from the payroll.

In future, Foremen noticing that any employee has made no movement for a period of two hours or more, are asked to investigate, as it is almost impossible to distinguish between death and the natural inertia of some employees. Foremen are cautioned to make a careful test, such as holding a paypacket in front of the suspected corpse. Care should be exercised however, with the paypacket, as there have been cases where the natural instinct is so deeply ingrained that the hand of the corpse has made spasmodic clutching movements, even after rigor mortis has set in.

N O T I C E

TO: All Employees over 40

SUBJECT: Early Retirement Programme

As a result of inflation, as well as a declining workload, Management must, of necessity, take steps to reduce the current workforce. A 'Reduction of Employees' programme has been devised which seems most equitable under the circumstances.

Under this plan, older employees will be placed in early retirement thus permitting the retention of employees who represent the future of the Company.

Therefore, a programme to phase out the older personnel (over 40) by the end of the current financial year will be put into effect immediately. The programme will be known as 'RAPE' (Retirement, Aged Personnel, Early). Employees who are 'RAPED' will be given the opportunity to seek other jobs within the system – provided that, while they are 'RAPED' they request a review of their employment status before actual retirement takes place.

This phase of the programme will be known as 'SCREW' (Survey of Capabilities of Retired Early Workers). All employees who have been 'RAPED' and 'SCREWED' may apply for a final review.

This phase will be known as 'STUFFED' (Study of Termination or Use For Further Education and Development).

Programme policy dictates that employees may be 'RAPED' once, 'SCREWED' twice, but can get 'STUFFED' as many times as the Management sees fit.

                    P. E. Dumdart
                    Rape Relations Office

1st July, 1975.

NEW CONDITIONS OF EMPLOYMENT

ABSENTEEISM

Due to the increase in absenteeism during the past year, it has become necessary to put the following rules and procedures into operation:-

1. SICKNESS

NO EXCUSE, and the Department will no longer accept your doctor's certificate as proof of illness. We believe that if you are able to attend the Doctor's Surgery, you are well enough to come to work.

2. DEATH (Other than your own)

There is NO EXCUSE. There is nothing you can do for them, and henceforth no time off will be allowed for funerals.

However, in case this should cause some hardship to some of our employees, there are those who might care to note that on your behalf the Department has supplied a scheme in conjunction with the Local Council for lunchtime funerals, thereby ensuring that no time off is necessary.

3. VISITS TO THE TOILET

Far too much time is spent in this particular practice.

In future the procedure will be that all personnel shall go in alphabetical order, e.g. those with the Surname beginning with the letter 'A' will go from 9.30 - 9.45, those beginning with 'B' will go from 9.45 - 10.00 etc.

NOTE

Anyone not able to attend at their proper turn will have to wait until the following day when their turn comes round again.

For those of you who are unfortunate enough to have Surnames beginning with the letters 'X', 'Y' or 'Z' the Department will provide buckets.

4. LEAVE OF ABSENCE FOR ALL OPERATIONS

We wish to discourage any thoughts you may have of needing an operation and henceforth no leave of absence will be granted for hospital visits. The Department believe that as long as you are employed here you will need all of whatever you already have, and should not consider having any of it removed. We engaged you for your particular job with all your parts, and having any removed would mean that we would be getting less than we are paying for.

5. BEATH (YOUR OWN)

This will be accepted as an excuse. We should like TWO WEEKS notice however since we feel that it is your duty to train someone else to do your job.

M E M O

To : ALL EMPLOYEES   From : TRAINING DEPARTMENT

ADDITIONAL TRAINING FOR ALL STAFF

It is now, and always has been, the policy of this Company to assure
its employees are well trained. Through our SPECIAL HIGH INTENSITY
TRAINING, (S.H.I.T) for short, we have given our employees more
S.H.I.T. than any other Company in the area.

If any employee feels that he or she does not receive enough S.H.I.T.
on the job, or that he or she could advance to another position by
taking more S.H.I.T. please see your immediate supervisor.

If you graduate to the top of your list by taking all the S.H.I.T. on
the job that is given to you, you can then qualify for our supervisors
programme, COMPLETE RESPONSIBILITY ACTION PROGRAMME (C.R.A.P.) for short.

So to become a member of our management team, simply take all the S.H.I.T.
you can and then with all the additional C.R.A.P. you receive, you will
soon become one of the elite.

For a limited period only, the company is offering all employees the
chance to try our latest scheme ADVANCED SUPERVISORY STAFF HELPING OUR
LOYAL EMPLOYER (A.S.S.H.O.L.E.) for short.

So work hard, and you will find that the more S.H.I.T. you take and the
more C.R.A.P. you can handle will qualify you as an A.S.S.H.O.L.E. for
sure.

OPEN TO ALL STAFF. IF INTERESTED PLEASE SIGN AND RETURN

NAME ....

DEPARTMENT ....

                    SIGNED ....

TO ALL LONDON STAFF

TOILET FACILITIES AND PROCEDURES

The following are company guidelines regarding the newly refurbished toilet facilities and procedures for their use by London based staff.

TOILET FACILITY CARDS - General description

In order that the most efficient use be made of these facilities, a joint task force committee from Systems, Communications and Office Services are now ready to issue each Division with new Toilet Utilisation and Reporting Devices.

Toilet Utilisation and Reporting Devices will allow the user to gain entry to the facility, select the utilisation mode (there will be two types of cards generally available, a No 1 card and a No 2 card) according to the type of card being used and the card will also allow the user to exit outwith the facility. FROM TUESDAY 24 APRIL ONWARDS, THESE FACILITIES WILL NOT BE AVAILABLE FOR USE WITHOUT INSERTING A TOILET UTILISATION AND REPORTING DEVICE INTO THE ELECTRONIC LOCKING DEVICE.

TOILET FACILITY CARDS - Issuance procedures

The cards will be held by the Divisional Managing Directors. Staff wishing to make use of a facility should proceed immediately to the office of their DMD and make a request (verbal mode) for a Toilet Utilisation and Reporting Device. Staff should state clearly whether they wish to use a No 1 Card or a No 2 Card. Staff should note that No 2 Cards have an inbuilt automatic credit facility which will credit your cost center in case of non-usage due to constipation. If a member of staff is uncertain as to their request status, they may, on completion of a written request (in triplicate) ask for a No 3 Card. This allows the user to engage either No 1 or No 2 mode at their own discretion, in situ. However, access to No 3 cards will be strictly monitored.

If the card of their choice is being used by another divisional member of staff, their request will be logged in the computer terminals now being installed on each floor. When the card is free, the computer will automatically call their telephone extension. If their extension is not answered, the Tannoy system will call their name and Card No. IN NO CIRCUMSTANCES SHOULD STAFF WAIT FOR CARDS OUTSIDE THE OFFICE OF THEIR DMD.

TOILET FACILITY CARDS - Issuance procedures for visitors

As from April 24 this new system will apply to visitors as well as staff.

Visitors wishing to use Collins PLC facilities should report to Reception and make a request (verbal mode) for either a No 1 or a No 2 Card. A phrase book will be available for foreign visitors with no English and for Glasgow staff. Editorial staff should contact Alf Evans for the special procedures for best-selling authors. No 3 Cards will not be available to visitors. UNDER NO CIRCUMSTANCES SHOULD STAFF ATTEMPT TO OBTAIN CARDS FROM RECEPTION. Unauthorised use of visitors' cards will invalidate the computer monitoring system.

TOILET FACILITY CARDS Use before 9.15am and after 5.30pm

After hours facilities will be restricted to one facility per sex. These can be located on the 6th, 5th and 4th floors. Cards will be held and issued by the security staff personnel. No 3 Cards will not be available from the security staff for obvious reasons.

It is hoped that staff will co-operate with this new system. It will allow the Group to achieve great savings in its central paper buying and water resource usage allocation. The Group has made every effort to ensure that this system is as safe as possible but it cannot accept liability for any unfortunate situations which may arise due to an electrical power failure. Firemen's axes will be available for any staff who may wish to either make use of the facilities during a power failure or who may wish to exit the facilities during a power failure. The axes will be issued by Alf Evans.

GROUP SPECIAL FACILITIES TASK FORCE

A company chairman was given a ticket for a performance of
Schubert's Unfinished Symphony. He couldn't go, and passed on the
invitation to the company's work study consultant. The next
morning the chairman asked him how he enjoyed it, and instead of
a few plausible observations was handed a memorandum which read:

a) For considerable periods the four oboe players had nothing to
   do. The number should be reduced, and their work spread over
   the whole orchestra, thus eliminating peaks of inactivity

b) All 12 violins were playing identical notes; this seems
   unnecessary duplication, and the staff of this section should
   be drastically cut. If a large volume of sound is really
   required this could be obtained through an electronic amplifier.

c) Much effort was absorbed in playing demi-semiquavers. This
   seems an excessive refinement, and it is recommended that all
   notes should be rounded up to the nearest semiquaver. If this
   were done it would be possible to use trainees and lower grade
   operators.

d) No useful purpose is served by repeating with horns the passage
   that has already been handled by the strings.

If all such redundant passages were eliminated, the concert would
be reduced from two hours to 20 minutes. In fact if Schubert had
attended to these matters, he would probably have been able to finish
the symphony after all!

DEPARTMENT OF INLAND REVENUE,
NEW GOVERNMENT BUILDING,
RISSIK STREET,
JOHANNESBURG.

NOTICE OF INCOME TAX.

Payment effective from 1st April, 1985.

TO ALL MALE TAX PAYERS.

GENTLEMEN,

The only thing the present goverment has not yet taxed is your
JOHN THOMAS, mainly because 98% of the time your JOHN THOMAS is
out of work; and the other 2% of the time it is in a hole.

Moreover, it has two dependants who are both nuts.

Accordingly, beginning 1st April 1985, your JOHN THOMAS will be
taxed according to SIZE - using the JOHN THOMAS CHART LIST below
to determine your category.

Please insert the information on Page 2, Section B, Line 2 of
your INLAND REVENUE TAX FORM.

Yours faithfully,

....
JOCK STRAP.
INSPECTOR OF TAXES.

              --- JOHN THOMAS CHART LIST ---

              10" to 12"   LUXURY TAX
               8" to 10"   POLE TAX
               6" to 8"   PRIVILEGE TAX
               4" to 6"   NUISANCE TAX

NOTE:

Anyone under 4" is eligible for rebate. Please do not request any
extensions.

Males exceeding 12" should file under CAPITAL GAIN.

Information to be inserted below, ...

If desired, a similar letter in the other offical language will be
sent.

A GUIDE TO EMPLOYEE PERFORMANCE APPRAISALS

Performance factor	Far exceeds job requirements	Exceeds job requirements	Meets job requirements	Needs some improvement	Below minimum requirements
Ability	Leaps over tall buildings with a single bound	Leaps over tall building after a running start	Can only leap over buildings without spires	Crashes into buildings when attempting to jump	Cannot recognise buildings - much less jump
Speed	Faster than light	Faster than bullet	As fast as a bullet	Would you believe a slow bullet?	Wounds self with bullet when attempting to shoot
Perseverance	Stronger than an elephant	Stronger than a bull	As strong as a bull	Thinks like a bull	Smells like a bull
Resourcefulness	Walks on water constantly	Walks on water occasionally	Washes with water	Drinks water	Passes water in emergencies
Communication.	Talks with God	Talks with Angels	Talks to himself	Argues with himself	Loses arguments with himself

Shearring Scott Limited

JP.21

ARMY GRATUITY ACCEPTANCE REPORT

1. NAME OF RECIPIENT OF GRATUITY: _____

2. GRADE (if civilian): _____
   BANK (while it lasts): _____
   SERIAL NO: _____

3. ORGANIZATION & LOCATION: _____

4. TELEPHONE NO: _____

5. DATE GRATUITIES ACCEPTED _____
   Was Gratuity solicited: ( ) Yes ( ) No

6. LOCATION:
   City _____
   State _____
   Country _____

7. GIVER: _____
   (Including nationality; i.e., Russian, Chinese, etc.)

8. TYPE OF GRATUITY ACCEPTED:
   a. Food and Beverage
      ( ) Drink(s) ( ) Drink(s) ( ) Drink(s)
      ( ) Lunch ( ) Dinner ( ) Breakfast

   b. Lodging/Accommodations
      ( ) Hotel/Motel   ( ) Private Boudoir
      ( ) Bordello   ( ) Corporate Pleasure
      ( ) Yacht   Dome
                        ( ) Other

   c. Narcotics
      ( ) Cigar(s)/cigarette(s) (Including light?)
      ( ) Marijuana ( ) Opium
      ( ) Heroin   ( ) Cocaine
      ( ) Morphine   ( ) Aphrodisiac (Specify)

   d. Companionship
      Type   Rating   Telephone
      ( ) Blonde(s)   ( ) Good   _____
      ( ) Brunette(s)   ( ) Better
      ( ) Redhead(s)   ( ) Wow!
      ( ) Homosexual(s)

   e. Miscellaneous
      ( ) Airplane model (missiles, rockets, systems, space capsules,
          satellites also applicable).
      ( ) Tie Clasp(s)   ( ) Calendar(s)   Pen(s)
                                           ( ) Ballpoint
      Pictures   ( ) Other
      ( ) Framed ( ) Unframed

   f. Other
      (Specify: e.g., vicuna, stereo, etc.) _____

      DISTRIBUTION:
      Orig: DOD Info Ofc
      1st cy: House Armed Svcs. Comm.
      2nd cy: Internal Revenue Services
      3rd cy: FBI
      4th cy: WCTU
      5th cy: Drew Pearson
      6th cy: Republican National Committee

9. Acceptance of the above gratuity is in the best
   interest of the United States Government
   because it:
   ( ) Increases Combat Effectiveness
                                    _____
                                    SIGNATURE
   ( ) Improves Morale
   ( ) Fights Poverty
   ( ) Strikes a Blow for Freedom

   FOR ADMINISTRATIVE USE ONLY:
   Recommended Action:
   ( ) Court Martial/Discharge ( ) Promotion
   ( ) Obtain as Personal Aide ( ) Transfer to NASA

THE COMMENCEMENT OF THE NEW LABOUR LAWS
PUBLISHED IN 1852

1. Godliness, Cleanliness, and Punctuality, are the necessities of a good business.

2. This firm has reduced the hours of work, and the clerical staff will now only have to be present between the hours of 7 a.m. and 7 p.m. on weekdays (6).

3. Daily prayers will be held each morning in the main office. The clerical staff will be present.

4. Clothing must be of a sober nature. The clerical staff will not disport themselves in raiments of bright colours, nor will they wear hose, unless in good repair.

5. Overshoes and top-coats may not be worn in the office, but neck scarves and headwear may be worn in inclement weather.

6. A stove is provided for the benefit of the clerical staff. Coal and wood must be kept in the locker. It is recommended that each member of the clerical staff bring four pounds of coal each day during cold weather.

7. No member of the clerical staff shall leave the room without the permission of Mr Rogers. The calls of nature are permitted, and clerical staff may use the garden below the second gate. This area must be kept in good order.

8. No talking is allowed during business hours.

9. The craving for tobacco, or spirits is a human weakness and, as such, is forbidden to all members of the clerical staff.

10. Now that the hours of business have been drastically reduced, the partaking of food is allowed between 11.30 a.m. and noon, but work will not, on any account cease.

11. Members of the clerical staff will provide their own pens. A new sharpener is available on application to Mr Rogers.

12. Mr Rogers will nominate a senior clerk to be responsible for the cleanliness of the main office, and the private office, and all boys and juniors will report to him forty minutes before prayers, and will remain after closing hours for similar work. Brushes, brooms, scrubbers, and soap are provided by the Owners.

13. The new increased weekly wages are as hereunder:

Junior boys (up to 11 years)	1s. 4d.
Boys (up to 14 years)	2s. 1d.
Juniors	4s. 8d.
Junior Clerks	8s. 7d.
Clerks	10s. 9d.
Senior Clerks (after 15 years service)	21s. 0d.

NOTE The Company recognises the generosity of the new Labour Laws but will expect a great rise in output of work to compensate for these near-Utopian conditions.

CARTOON TIME

SAVE
WATER!

"PAY ATTENTION GOLDAMIT, I SAID THE SCHMIDT HOUSE!"

AS PROPOSED BY THE PROJECT SPONSOR

AS SPECIFIED IN THE PROJECT REQUEST

AS DESIGNED BY THE SENIOR SYSTEMS ANALYST

AS PRODUCED BY THE PROGRAMMERS

AS INSTALLED AT THE USER'S SITE

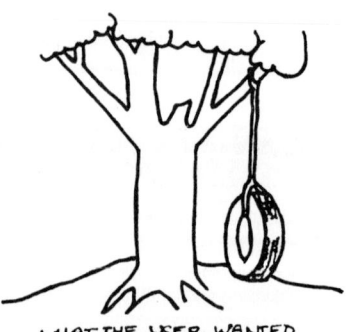

WHAT THE USER WANTED

GRAB THE VINE
JANE — THE VINE

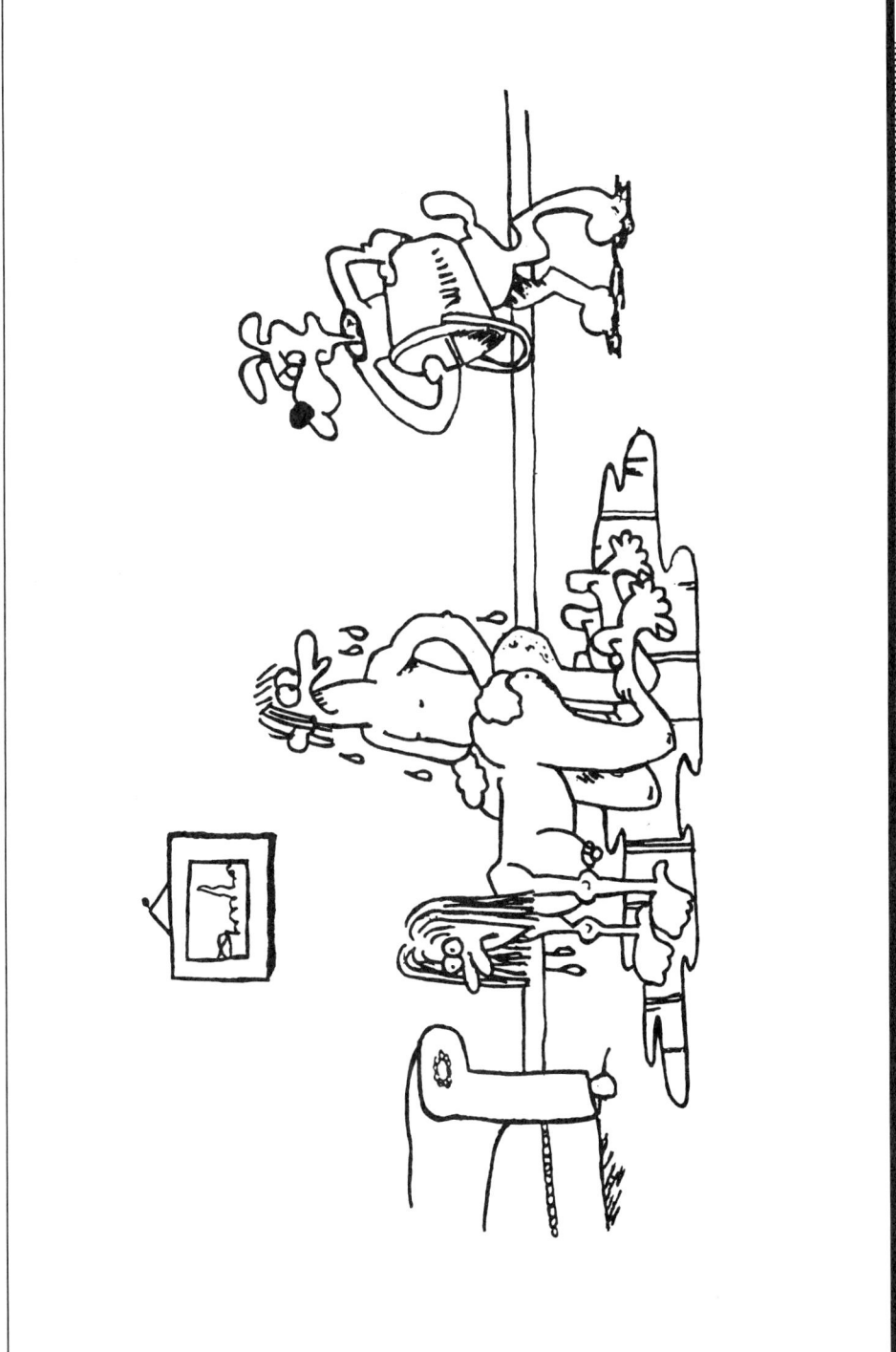

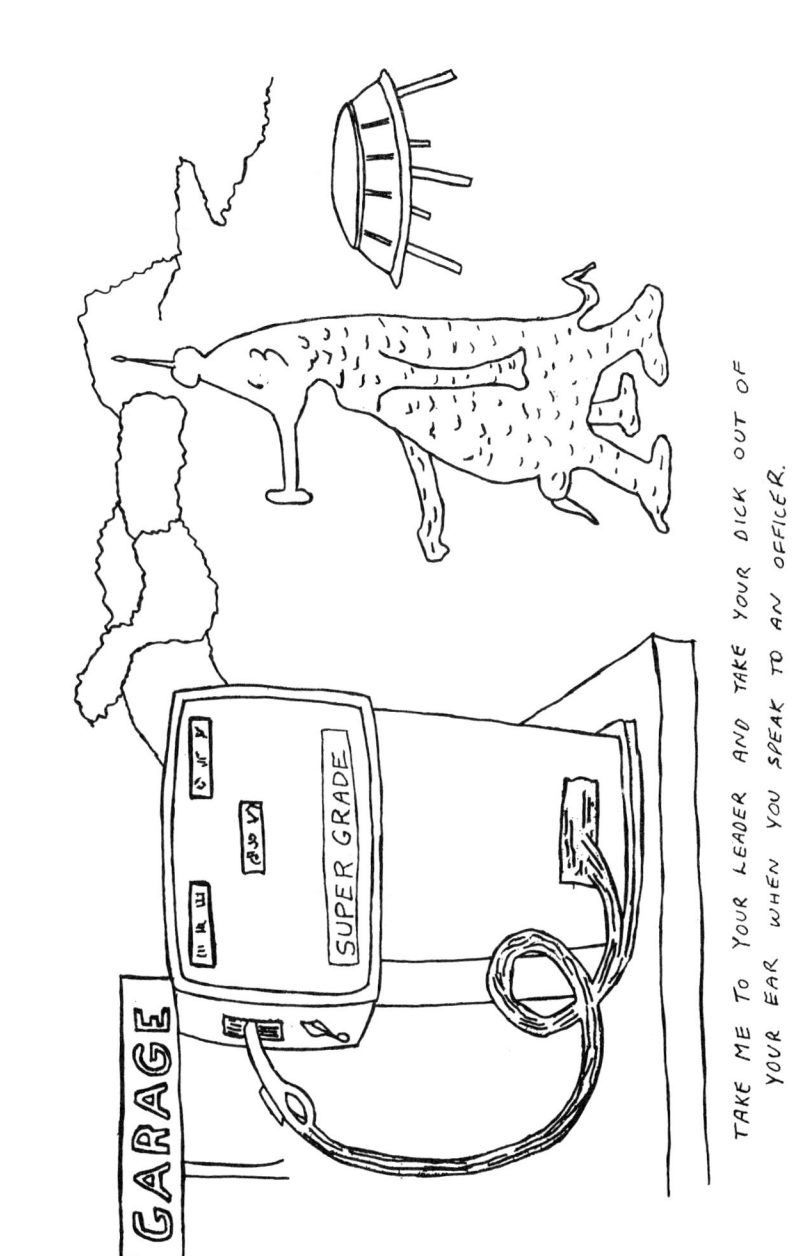

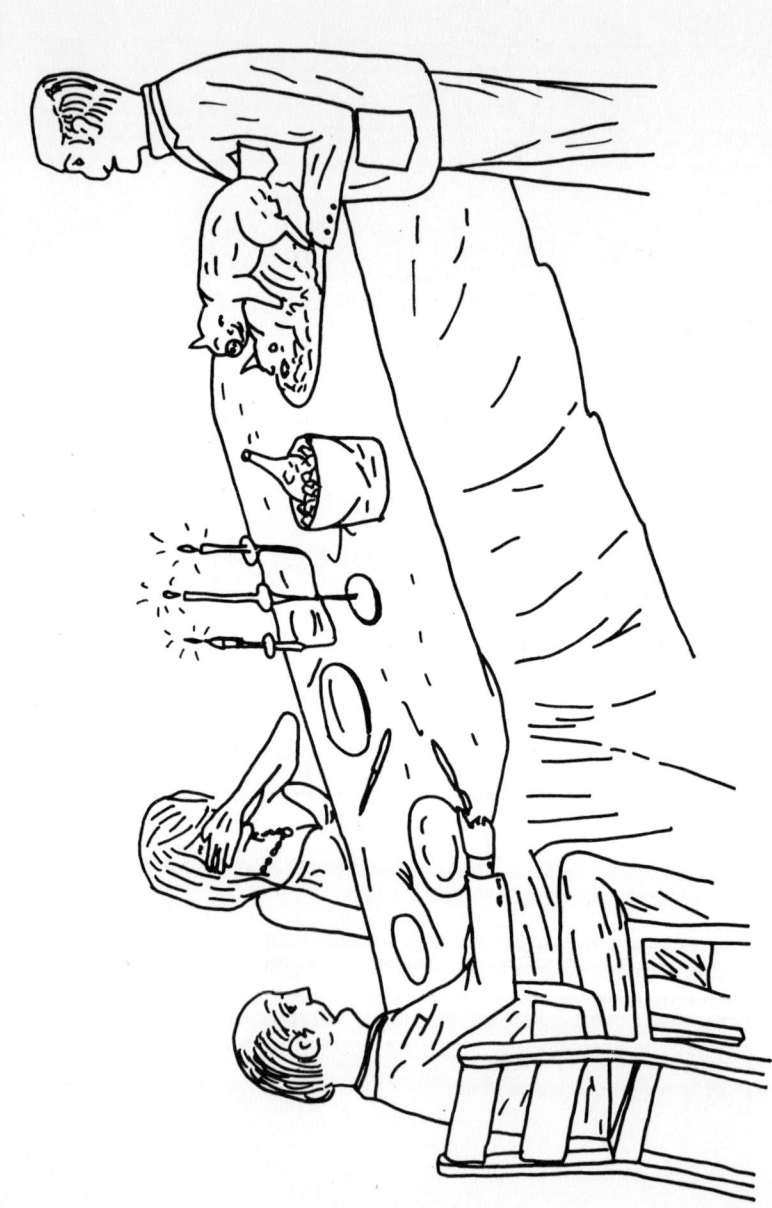

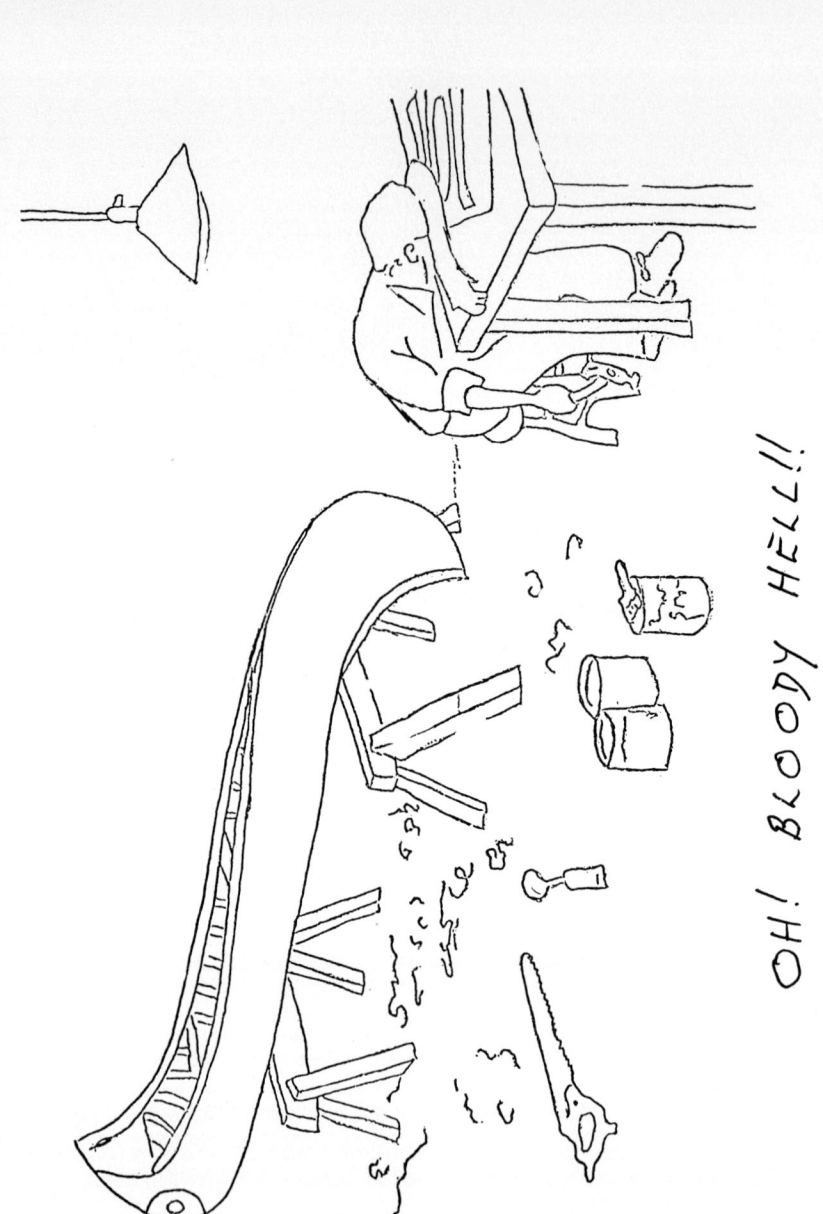

QUESTIONS AND ANSWERS

SO THAT'S WHY LITTLE
BOYS CAN RUN FASTER
THAN LITTLE GIRLS.....
"BALL BEARINGS!!!
(AND A STICK SHIFT!)

CRICKET
(AS EXPLAINED TO A FOREIGN VISITOR)

YOU HAVE TWO SIDES ONE OUT IN THE FIELD AND ONE IN.

EACH MAN THAT'S IN THE SIDE THAT'S IN GOES OUT AND WHEN HE'S OUT HE COMES IN AND THE NEXT MAN GOES IN UNTIL HE'S OUT.

WHEN THEY ARE ALL OUT THE SIDE THAT'S OUT COMES IN AND THE SIDE THAT'S BEEN IN GOES OUT AND TRIES TO GET THOSE COMING IN OUT.

SOMETIMES YOU GET MEN STILL IN AND NOT OUT.

WHEN BOTH SIDES HAVE BEEN IN AND OUT INCLUDING THE NOT OUT'S.

THAT'S THE END OF THE GAME.

HOWZAT!

PSYCHOLOGICAL STUDIES OF TYPES OF MEN YOU MEET IN PUBLIC TOILETS

EXCITABLE	Pants half twisted around - can't find hole, rips pants.
SOCIABLE	Joins friends in pee, if he has to go or not.
NOSY	Looks into next urinal to see how other man is doing.
CROSS-EYED	Looks into next urinal left, pees into one in centre.
TIMID	Cannot urinate if someone is watching. Flushes urinal as if he had gone.
INDIFFERENT	All urinals are in use, pees in sink.
CLEVER	No hands, shows off by fixing tie, looks around, pees on floor.
WORRIED	Is not sure of what he has been doing, makes a quick inspection.
FRIVOLOUS	Plays stream up and down and across urinal - tries to hit fly.
ABSENT-MINDED	Opens waistcoat, pulls out tie, pees in trousers.
SNEAK	Farts silently while leaking - acts very innocent - knows that the man in the next stall will be blamed.
DISGUSTED	Stands for a while, gives up, walks away.
CHILDISH	Leaks directly into urinal bottom, likes to see bubbles.
PATIENT	Stands very close for a long time waiting, reads newspaper with free hand.
EFFICIENT	Waits until he has to crap then does both.
TOUGH	Bangs dong against urinal to dry it off.
FAT	Has to stand back to take long blind shot at urinal, misses, pees in shoe.
LITTLE	Stands on box, falls in, drowns.
WITHDRAWN	Places foot in urinal, pees down leg, thus eliminating noise.
DRUNK	Holds left thumb in right hand - pees in trousers.
IMPATIENT	Always in a hurry, pees down back of man using urinal right in front of him.

TYPES OF GIRLS IN POWDER ROOM

CAUTIOUS GIRL: Has heard of many girls contacting "V.D." from toilet seats, lifts seat, straddles bowl, leans over to flush toilet and pees over her brand new nylons.

INDIFFERENT GIRL: Rushes in, lifts dress, pulls panty crotch aside and just lets go, sounds like a bucket of water being poured out of a third story window.

WORRIED GIRL: A week past due, visits powder room every hour, sits down, uses toilet paper looks for encouraging red design, walks out biting nails.

PRESIDENT'S SECRETARY: Has key to our private can, walks in, gives other girls the "High-Hat." This type farts louder than a fire-cracker and stinks worse than a goat.

SLOPPY GIRL: Pees all over front of toilet seat, is halfway out of powder room before she notices panties down over her ankles.

SOPHISTICATED GIRL: Seldom wears pants. Never knows when she will meet a male friend.

BASHFUL GIRL: Looks under privy doors, to see if anyone else is in powder room. If not alone sits down, holds hand on toilet seat flush for constant flow of water. Pees quietly, coughs, hums and ends up with a loud fart after water has ceased flushing. She walks out blushing.

ACROBATIC: Stands up with one foot on toilet seat and in this position emits a straight forward stream. This type about as tight as the inside of a size "8" derby hat.

CROSS-EYED: Sits with one cheek on side of seat and in this position pees all over the floor. Usually wears galoshes on her visits to the can.

FRIVOLOUS: Lets stream go in squirts to the tune of "Little Toot" whistles while she wee-wees.

LITERARY: Always takes current book of the month to powder room. Sits on can and reads. Blames "Forever Amber" for her piles.

BIG TIMER: Always leaves toilet door open while she chats and brags to other girls about the guy she took over the night before. Shows girls panties with black lace edging and "Welcome" embroidered on crotch. Has never been in bed with a man.

ABSENT-MINDED: Forgets she has snuggies, pees herself before she can get the damn things off.

THE DRUMS OF FU PERSON CHU;

or , a Vocabulary for the Liberated Woman

WORDS:
Garbage person
Space person
Tribesperson
Rifleperson
Ombudsperson
Good Humor Person
Linesperson
Midshipperson
Fisherperson
Camera person
Brakeperson
Letterperson
Pullperson
Lawperson
Middleperson
He-person
Gentleperson
Nobleperson
Clergyperson
Lady's person
Dirty Old Person
Penpersonship
Personikin
Ploughperson
Gingerbread person
Fairy Godperson
Underpersonned
Personning
Person-slaughter
Person power
Personly
Person trap
Personopause
Longshore person
Seaperson
First base person
Bandsperson
Family person
Business person
Swordsperson
Con-person
China person
Drafts person
Klans person
Ruddle person
Personhood
Organization person
Hit person
Minute person
Yes-person
Cavalry person
Boogey person
Pitch person
Holdup person

Bag person
Highway person
Sand person
Head person
Milk person
Mail person
Post person
Repair person
Ape person
Air person
Wing person
Watch person
Yeoperson
Superperson
Hang person
Ad person
Gun person
Handy person
Freshperson
Henchperson
Chairperson
Workperson
Personhold
Personkind
Charperson
Horseperson
Mad person
Police person
Fireperson
Personhandle

IMPORTANT TITLES:
Bird Person of Alcatraz
The Iceperson Commeth
Isle of Person
Frankenstein Meets the Wolfperson
Person of La Mancha (Personcha?)
I am Person!
No Person is an Island
Descent of Person

CLASSIC PHRASES:
Person the Life Boats!
Person Overboard!
Clothes Don't Make the Person!
Person Alive!
Friends, Ro-Persons, Countrypersons....
One small step for person....
    One giant step for personkind.

NB: The editors admit that the word "person"
is considered chauvinistic in certain circles,
the preferred word being "perchild." Should
Liberated Women generally agree to substitute
perchild for person, we will consider this
document inoperative and rewrite the English
language yet again.

LOW CALORIE DIET

(You are guaranteed to lose weight.)

Monday: **Breakfast** Weak tea
Lunch 1 bouillon cube in ¼ cup of diluted water
Dinner 1 pigeon thigh
3 oz. prune juice (gargle only)

Tuesday: **Breakfast** Scraped crumbs from burned toast
Lunch 1 doughnut hole (without sugar)
1 glass of dehydrated water
Dinner 2 grains of corn meal (broiled)

Wednesday: **Breakfast** Boiled out stains of tablecloth
Lunch ½ doz. poppy seeds
Dinner Bees knees and mosquitos knuckles sauteed in vinegar

Thursday: **Breakfast** Shredded eggshell skins
Lunch 1 Belly button from a navel orange
Dinner 3 eyes from Irish potato (diced)

Friday: **Breakfast** 2 lobster antennae
Lunch 1 guppy fin
Dinner Fillet of soft shell crab claw

Saturday: **Breakfast** 4 chopped banana seeds
Lunch Broiled butterfly liver
Dinner Jelly fish vertebrae à la bookbinder

Sunday: **Breakfast** Pickled hummingbird tongue
Lunch Prime ribs of tadpole
Aroma of empty custard pie plate
Dinner Tossed paprika and (1) clover leaf salad

Note: All meals to be eaten under microscope to avoid extra portions.

MAKE LOVE, NOT FAT

The Sensual Dieter's Guide to
Weight Loss During SEX

SEXUAL ACTIVITY   **CALORIES BURNED**

Activity	Calories
Lust	5
Listening to music: light classical	1
rock	5
Embracing and hugging	4
Kissing: regular	3
passionate	11
Arousal	8
Petting: light	$3\frac{1}{2}$
heavy	8
Removing clothes in winter	15
in summer	2
Stage fright	17
General foreplay (nothing too fancy)	12
Cunnilingus	22
Fellatio	22
Achieving erection for the man	1
for the woman	34
Fumbling around	$6\frac{1}{4}$
Finding a more comfortable position	11
Moaning	3
Giggling	4
Laughing	5
Insertion if man is ready	$\frac{1}{2}$
if woman is not	60
Intercourse moderate	25
heavy	48
incoherent convulsions	92
Orgasm real	40
faked	143
Getting a towel	10
Avoiding the wet spot	14
Sleeping	8
Showering	12
Expressing thanks	$2\frac{1}{2}$

Supplementary Activities

Anxiety	8
Immature ejaculation	0
Premature ejaculation	6
Cursing	4
Begging for another chance	14
Putting on prophylactic with erection	3
without erection	83

*3500 calories burned = one pound of weight lost

DEFINITION OF AN EXECUTIVE

An Executive is a person who is able to decide what is
to be done and be able to tell someone how to do it.

To listen to reasons why it should not be done, or
should be done by someone else or done in a different
way.

To follow it up to see if the thing has been done.

To discover that it has not been done and to ask why.

To listen to excuses from the person who should have
done it.

To follow up and see if the work has been done properly
at last only to discover it was done incorrectly.

To point out how it should have been done.

To conclude that so long as the work has been done to
let it stay as it is.

To wonder if there is any time to get rid of the person
who cannot do a thing right, but also to reflect that
he probably has a wife and ten children and that anyway
someone else would do it just as badly if not worse.

To consider how much simpler and better the work would
have been done if he had done it himself in the first
place.

To reflect sadly that he could have done it right in
twenty minutes and that as things turned out he has
had to spend two days to find out why it has taken
three weeks for someone else to do it the wrong way.

THE DRINKING MAN'S SOLUTION

Since you will insist on drinking have you considered the possibilities of running your own bar and drinking mostly at home for which you need no licence?

1. Current bar prices are around 35p for a single scotch
2. A standard bottle of scotch contains 30 tots
3. If you give your wife £52.80p she can buy a crate of 12 bottles to start things going
4. Pay her 35p per tot and in 12 days (at a bottle a day) she will have £126.   £52.80 for another crate and £73.20 to bank.

In this way your wife can accumulate capital at around £2,196 per year and, assuming you may last another 15 years, she can then expect to have over £40,000 invested. This will enable her, after settling your funeral expenses, to pay off the mortgage, educate the children, marry a decent man and forget she ever knew a bum like you.

H.G.V. LORRY DRIVERS' HIGHWAY CODE TEST

QUESTIONS	ANSWERS
1. When should you use head lights?	— To warn your mates of speed traps.
2. When do you overtake on the left?	— When the b------ in front won't move over.
3. What documents do you take on the road?	— Daily Mirror, Sun, Playboy, Forum.
4. When must you stop?	— To have a slash, leg over or tot of brandy.
5. Where should you not park?	— Outside the house of the women you're having it off with.
6. What do you expect to see on a rural road?	— Rural tarmac.
7. How many types of pedestrian crossings are there?	— Two. Those who make it, those who don't.
8. What is the correct procedure for overtaking on motorway?	— Foot hard down, eyes shut and smile.
9. When should you use the fast lane on motorway?	— When going home on a promise.
10. What do you do in the event of a breakdown on motorway?	— Leave the f------ thing and hitch a lift home.
11. What does a yellow box junction mean?	— They have run out of white paint.
12. What do broken white lines mean on the road?	— Careless navvies.
13. What does the Highway Code say about tyres?	— Use only round ones.
14. When can you cross double yellow lines?	— After 9 pints, 2 vodkas and 1 whisky.
15. How do you avoid drowsiness on the motorway?	— Goose the hitch hiker.
16. What must you check when leaving a building site?	— That you have enough timber under the sheet for a new kitchen cabinet.
17. What do double yellow lines on the road side mean?	— A Chinese take-away.
18. Where do you situate your danger triangle when broken down?	— Up the transport manager's jacksey.

CONGRATULATIONS ON PASSING YOUR H.G.V. TEST

TO:

SUBJECT: LONDON'S NINE NEWSPAPERS

THE TIMES   –   Read by the people who run
                          the country.

DAILY MIRROR   –   Read by the people who think
                          they run the country.

GUARDIAN   –   Read by people who think they
                          ought to run the country.

MORNING STAR   –   Read by people who think the
                          country ought to be run by
                          another country.

DAILY MAIL   –   Read by the wives of the people
                          who run the country.

FINANCIAL TIMES   –   Read by the people who own the
                          country.

DAILY EXPRESS   –   Read by the people who think
                          the country ought to be run the
                          way it used to be run.

DAILY TELEGRAPH   –   Read by the people who think
                          it still is.

THE SUN   –   Their readers don't care who
                          runs the fucking country, as
                          long as they've got big tits!

AID TO CENTRAL LONDON

The following instructions are to be brought to the attention of all officers being supplied as 'AID'.

Dress:- No 2 Trousers (Pressed), Boots (Shone), Reinforced Helmets, truncheons and whistles must be carried.

Non-authorised clothing:- Crash Helmets, Steel capped boots, jogging shoes and squad ties will not be worn. Inspectors in charge of serials will search their officers at time of parade to ensure that no officers have concealed six foot scaffold poles or pick-axe handles in their trunchon pockets. Protective clothing: The only protective clothing allowed is a police long service and good conduct medal, which should be worn in a prominent position so as to allow the local youth to identify old policemen who they do not like from young policemen who they like even less.

The following practices have been noted and should cease forthwith: Missiles thrown at police should not be picked up and thrown back. Once the missile has hit the ground it is deemed 'out of play'. However, missiles in mid-flight may be headed back, although prior to this helmets should be removed to prevent damage to the helmet plate. The practice, especially amongst members of shield serials of whooping like cowboys and indians, and 'beating of truncheons' on riot shields must cease - as this tends to frighten and intimidate rioters.

The practice of 'blacking up' faces is definitely inappropriate in the present conflict.

Sirens on police vehicles should not be used as these have been confused with air raid warnings, causing an influx of residents into the underground stations.

Members of TR KERMITS MARAUDERS must no longer absail into Brixton Broadway from the roof of Woolworths as the manager complains that this is damaging his burnt paintwork.

Officers who are unfortunately set alight by petrol bombs should not run down the road screaming, but should lay down with dignity and await their turn to be put out.

Officers attempting to obtain more than one permitted ham roll will be dealt with most severely by being returned to their divisions and not be allowed to attend future riots.

Before leaving for Brixton, Inspectors should brief their men on local customs and traditions. It has been statistically proved that the young of the area are six times more helpful than the youngsters in the rest of the country in carrying ladies bags - this action leads to about sixty misunderstandings a week.

Brixton like the rest of the country has its take-away shops, only here the service includes: Jewellers, Burtons, Woolworths, and Camera shops. In fact most shops can be regarded as 'in the scheme'. The public houses are all 'Free Houses'.

The youngsters of the area hold celebrations similar to our Guy Fawkes night, when Pubs, Shops, Homes and policemen are set alight.

Finally, should any elderly residents approach officers complaining of being assaulted or mugged, they should be closely questioned to ascertain if they are trying to start a riot.

James Larking. A.B.C.

THE HEALTH EDUCATION DIVISION IN MALAWI SET AN EXAMINATION FOR AFRICAN STUDENTS AND THESE ARE SOME OF THE ANSWERS FROM VARIOUS EXAMINATION PAPERS:

1. Benjamin Franklin produced electricity by rubbing cats backwards.
2. Three kinds of blood vessels are arteries, veins and caterpillars.
3. A thermometer is an instrument for raising temperatures.
4. To remove air from a flask, fill the flask quick with water, tip the water out and put the cork on quick.
5. A litre is a nest of young animals.
6. A vacuum is a U tube with a flask at each end.
7. The cuckoo does not lay its own eggs.
8. Typhoid fever may be prevented by fascination.
9. Algebra was the wife of Euclid.
10. An axiom is a thing that is so visible that it is not necessary to see it.
11. A circle is a line which meets its other end without ending.
12. An example of animal breeding is the farmer who mated a bull that gave a great deal of milk with a bull with good meat.
13. By self pollination a farmer may get a flock of long-haired sheep.
14. A super saturated solution is one that holds more than it can hold.
15. The hydro gets food into its mouth by descending upon its prey and pushing it into its mouth with its testicles.
16. A person should take a bath once in summer time and not quite so often in winter time.
17. For fainting, rub the person's chest, or if a lady, rub her arm above the hand.
18. For fractures, to see if the limb is broken, wiggle it gently back and forth.
19. For dog bite, put the dog away for several days, if it has not recovered then kill it.
20. To remove dust from the eye, pull the eye over the nose.
21. For nose bleed, put the nose lower than the body.
22. For head colds, use an agonizer to spray nose until it drops into your throat.
23. For snake bite, bleed the wound and rape the victim in a blanket for shock.
24. For asphyxiation, apply artificial respiration until the patient is dead.
25. It is well known that a deceased body warps the mind.
26. The cerebrum is a cavity in the head.
27. Blood flows down one leg and up the other.
28. Parallel lines do not meet unless you bend one or both of them.
29. A magnet is something you find in a bad apple.
30. Geometry teaches us to bisex angles.

HOW YOU CAN TELL IT'S GOING TO BE A ROTTEN DAY

- You wake up face down on the pavement.
- You put your bra on backwards and it fits better.
- You call "The Samaritans" and they put you on hold.
- You see a "60 Minutes" news team waiting in your office.
- Your birthday cake collapses from the weight of the candles.
- You want to put on the clothes you wore home from the party and they're not anywhere around.
- You turn on the news and they're showing emergency routes out of the city.
- Your twin sister forgot your birthday.
- You wake up and discover your waterbed has broken; then you realise you don't have a waterbed.
- Your car horn accidentally goes off and remains stuck as you follow a group of "Hells Angels" on the motorway.
- Your wife wakes up feeling amorous and you have a headache.
- Your boss tells you not to bother to take off your coat.
- The bird singing outside your window is a buzzard.
- You walk to work and find your dress is stuck in the back of your tights.
- Your blind date turns out to be your ex-wife.
- You put both your contact lenses in the same eye.
- Your pet rock snaps at you.
- Your wife says, "Good Morning, Bill" and your name is George.
- You call your answering services; they tell you it's none of your business.
- The woman you are seeing on the side begins to look like your wife.
- Your kids tell you, "Did you know that it is almost impossible to flush a grapefruit down the toilet."
- You're driving to work smoking a cigarette. At a stop sign, you drop the lit cigarette between your legs. As you panic searching for it, a full bus pulls up alongside your car.

SONGS FOR OUR TIMES

ODE TO THE FOUR-LETTER WORDS

Let us banish the use of the four-lettered words,
Whose meanings are never obscure;
The Angles, the Saxons, those bawdy old birds,
Were vulgar, obscene and impure.
But cherish the use of the wheedling phrase
Which never says quite what you mean;
You'd better be known for hypocritic ways,
Than be vulgar, impure or obscene.

When nature is calling, plain speaking is out,
If the ladies, God bless them, are milling about,
Please temper your language with words of a sense,
That will tell them your plight without giving offense.
You may wee-wee, make water, or empty the glass,
Shake dew off the lily, make water or pass.
But please, please remember, if you would know bliss,
That only in Shakespeare do characters ------------.

A woman has bosoms, a bust or a breast,
Those lily-white swellings that bulge 'neath her vest.
Call them towers of ivory, sheaves of new wheat,
Or in moments of passion, ripe apples to eat.
You may speak of her nipples as fingers of fire
And there's hardly a question of rousing her ire.
But, by Raphael's beard, she'll throw several fits
If you speak of them roundly, as good, honest --------.

It's a haven of joy that you're thinking of now,
A warm, tender pasture awaiting the plough.
It's a quivering pigeon caressing your hand,
The National Anthem, it makes a man stand.
Or maybe a flower, a grotto, a well,
The hope of the world, a velvety hell;
But friend, heed this warning, beware the affront
Of aping the Saxons; don't call it a ------------.

Though the lady repel your advance, she'll be kind
As long as you intimate what's on your mind.
You can tell her you're hungry, you need to be swung,
Or ask her to see how your etchings are hung.
You may mention the ashes that need to be hauled,
And even at moments the word "lay's" not too bold.
But the moment you're forthright, get ready to duck,
For the girl isn't born who'll stand for Let's --------!"

So banish the words fair Elizabeth used
When she was a queen on the throne,
The modern maid's virtue is easily bruised
By the four-lettered words used alone.
Let your morals be loose as an alderman's vest,
If your language is always obscure;
Today, not the act, but the word is the test,
Of the vulgar, obscene and impure.

                                        —Anon.

ODE TO SARAH JANE

Here is the tale of Sarah Jane,
Whose charm and looks could drive insane.
Whose aura flows in pure delight,
A truly fine and sensual sight.

She charmed the men of Aylesbury Town,
Who always followed her around.
But poor Sarah Jane for true love sought,
Yet she failed to find a true consort.

She travelled far to distant cities,
And men marvelled at her firm young titties.
Her slender body made to please,
And her slightly bowed but lovely knees.

Her grace and charm made men light headed,
It is said that those that she bedded,
Would never feel or be the same,
As before they met Sarah Jane.

And yet true love passed by still,
And Sarah Jane's heart grew ill.
The hopes, tattered, blue and faded,
No love for her but longing jaded.

And then as if through celestial glow,
Cupid's arrow struck its blow,
And Janey's life was lit with joy,
At the coming of a new found boy.

This man she found she gave her all,
She followed every beck and call.
Whether just a loving little kiss,
Or making love with sensual bliss.

But the light turned to darkest dark,
For out of the blue he did depart.
Yet even so she was left a present,
Of the love now gone but once so pleasant.

So the moral of this story to one and all,
If you are bitten by loves sweet call.
Beware of washing up and dirty socks,
But most of all a dose of pox.

MY LAST WILL

When I am dead
And in my grave,
No more pussy
Will I crave.

On my tombstone
Shall be written,
I had my share
And, I ain't shitten.

When I die bury me deep,
Make it simple,
Make it cheap.

On my tombstone shall be written,
Millions of drinks,
Went down my throat.

If you should pass by,
Where I lie,
Piss on me
I'm always dry.

Tombstone Territory

THE UNION OFFICIAL'S PRAYER

Grant me O Lord, the genius to explain to my Brothers and Sisters
the policies and plans of our great Union –
Even though no-one explains them to me.

Give to me the intelligence, the wisdom and the
knowledge to understand the new techniques
applicable to our industry so that I may evaluate
their impact on my Brothers and Sisters.

Even though no-one shows me these techniques,
No-one shows me how to evaluate them, and no-one is
quite sure if they are, in fact, of any value at all.

Give to me understanding that I may –
Forgive the apathetic member,
Cure the over-ambitious member,
Accept the views of the member who does nothing
until I have done something and then tells me how I
should have done it and what I should have done.

Make me formidable in debate, logical in argument,
fearless in confrontation: lawyer, actor,
mathematician, sage, philosopher, sociologist and
economist; pleading, cajoling, threatening,
belabouring, so that I may make the best of a
good case and a good case from no case at all.

Teach me, O Lord to stand with both feet firmly on the ground
Even though I haven't a leg to stand on.
Oh Lord, let my brothers and sisters see the future as a great
Brotherhood of men and sisterhood of Women and
When they at last believe in it,
Give me the physical strength to stop the punch-ups that ensue.

Lord, I am a Union Official: I pray you, in your
Infinite Wisdom see my need for all these things and
in your Great Mercy, grant them to me.

WHEN I HAVE THEM LORD – MOVE OVER

AND PIGS FLEW OVERHEAD

It was crisis day in the Commons
The house was hushed and still,
As a Member rose with a question
"Are we doomed to go downhill!"

"I am confident of an upturn"
The P.M. made reply:
"If workers' pay is held at bay
We'll all be home and dry."

"How true! How true!" cried the workers,
"Let's end this wicked strike,
We don't want a rise in wages,
They can stick it where they like."

"Thank God! Thank God!" sobbed the bosses,
"There's faith on the factory floor,
And now we've got this extra lot,
We'll give it to the poor!"

They filled their pockets with money,
And ran with eager feet,
Pressing their surplus profits
On people in the street.

They moved among the dole queues,
And boarded every bus,
With streaming eyes and heartfelt cries:
"You need it more than us!"

Soon all the people prospered,
And the devil became a saint,
Now that the sober unions,
Had exercised constraint.

And the cities were filled with singing,
And the sound of laughter spread,
As hand took hand in the golden land,
And pigs flew overhead.

ODE TO APPLICATIONS DEPARTMENT

1. The office is so stuffy
    It's difficult to breathe
    Oh isn't it a folly
    We cannot get no breeze.

2. We cannot get no fresh air
    It's always blooming hot
    There must be some air somewhere
    But we know where it's not.

3. We'd love to have a cooler
    A ventilator too
    Of one thing we are surer
    It's hotter in the Loo.

4. We got the double glazing
    To keep the noise out
    But also, we are saying
    It keeps fresh air without.

5. The windows that do open
    Are nineteen inches square
    We get no fresh air through them
    It really isn't fair.

6. Each window has it's own fan
    A roof fan of design
    They really could improve them
    Or should we all resign.

With acknowledgements to Ernie Wise and apologies
to the English language – like wot 'e wrote it.

P.S. Wot can be done about it
      The engineers did cry
      Close the Bastard place down
      The unaminous reply.

The Indispensable Man.

Some time when you're feeling important,
Some time when your ego's in bloom,
Some time when you take it for granted
You're the best qualified man in the room.

Some time when you feel that your going
Would leave an unfillable hole,
Just follow these simple instructions
And see how they humble your soul.

Take a bucket and fill it with water,
Put your hands in it up to your wrists.
Pull them out and the hole that remains
Is the measure of how you'll be missed.

You may splash all you please when you enter,
You may stir up the waters galore,
But stop and you'll find in a minute
That it looks just the same as before.

The moral of this is quite simple :-
You must do the best that you can,
Be proud of yourself, but remember
There is no indispensable man.

Prayer for Dieters

Lord, grant me the strength that I may not fall

   Into the clutches of cholesterol.

At polyunsaturates I'll never mutter

   For the road to Hell is paved with butter.

And cake is cursed and cream is awful

   And Satan is hiding in every waffle.

Beelzebub is a chocolate drop

   And Lucifer is a lollipop.

Teach me the evils of Hollandaise.

   Of pasta and gobs of mayonnaise.

And crisp fried chicken from the South,

   Lord, if you love me, shut my mouth!

DARWIN'S MISTAKE

Three monkeys sat in a coconut tree
Discussing things as they're said to be
Said one to the others "Now listen, you two
There's a certain rumour that can't be true,
That man descended from our noble race.
That very idea is a disgrace."

No Monkey ever deserted his wife,
Starved her babies or ruined her life.
And another thing you will never see
A monk build a fence around a coconut tree
And let the coconuts go to waste,
Forbidding all other monks to taste.

If I put a fence around this tree,
Starvation would force you to steal from me.
Here's another thing a monk won't do,
Go out at night and get on a stew,
And use a gun or club or knife
To take some other monkey's life.
Yes, man descended, the ornery cuss –
But, brother, he didn't descend from us.

                                        ANON

"GOOD MORNING"

BY

Donna Smith

Age 8 - 3rd Grade

The sun was shining brightly
And I could hardly wait
To ponder out my window
And gaze at my estate.

The breeze was blowing briskly
It made the flowers sway
The garden was enchanting
On this inspiring day.

My eyes fell on a little bird
With a beautiful yellow bill
I beckoned him to come and light
Upon my window sill.

I smiled at him cheerfully
And gave him a crust of bread
Then I quickly closed the window
And smashed its fucking head.

The Hierarchy of Power Semantics

In the beginning was the Plan and the Specification.
And the Plan was without form and the Specification it was void.
And darkness was on the face of the implementation team.
And they spake unto their leader, saying,
  "It is a crock of shit and it stinks to high heaven."

And it was the leader and it was the project head.
Now the leader spake unto the project head, saying,
  "It is a crock of faeces and intolerably malodorous."

And it was the project head and it was the department manager.
Now the project head spake unto his department manager, saying,
  "It is a container of excrement and its effluvium is very strong."

And it was the department manager and it was the product manager.
Now the department manager spake unto his product manager, saying,
  "It is a vessel of fertilizer of overpowering strength."

And it was the product manager and it was the centre manager.
Now the product manager spake unto his centre manager, saying,
  "It containeth that which aideth the growth of plants and strong it is."

And it was the centre manager and it was the director.
Now the centre manager spake unto his director, saying,
  "It promotes growth and it is very powerful."

And it was the director and it was the vice-president.
Now the director spake unto his vice-president, saying,
  "This powerful new product will promote the growth of the Company."

And the vice-president looked on the product and saw that it was good.

RETIREMENT *BLUES*

MY NOOKIE DAYS ARE OVER,
MY PILOT LIGHT IS OUT.
WHAT USED TO BE MY SEX APPEAL,
IS NOW MY WATER SPOUT.
TIME WAS WHEN OF ITS OWN ACCORD,
FROM MY TROUSERS IT WOULD SPRING.
BUT NOW I HAVE A FULL TIME JOB,
TO FIND THE BLASTED THING.
IT USED TO BE EMBARRASSING,
THE WAY IT WOULD BEHAVE.
FOR EVERY SINGLE MORNING,
IT WOULD STAND & WATCH ME SHAVE.
AS OLD AGE APPROACHES,
IT SURE GIVES ME THE BLUES,
TO SEE IT HANG ITS WITHERED HEAD
AND WATCH ME TIE MY SHOES.

TEA BREAK TALES

A couple, aged 67, went to the doctor's office. The doctor asked, "What can I do for you?" The man said, "Will you watch us have sexual intercourse?" The doctor looked puzzled but agreed; when the couple had finished, the doctor said, "There is nothing wrong with the way you have intercourse." And he charged them $10. This happened several weeks in a row. The couple would make an appointment, have intercourse, pay the doctor and leave.

Finally the doctor asked, "Just exactly what are you trying to find out?" The old man said, "We're not trying to find out anything. She is married and we can't go to her house. I am married and we can't go to my house. Holiday Inn charges $22; Hilton Hotel charges $27. We do it here for $10 and I get $8 back from Medicare for a visit to the doctor's office."

THE MISPLACED PAIR OF GLOVES

A young man wished to purchase a birthday present for his sweetheart and after consideration, he decided on a pair of gloves. Accompanied by his sister, they went to a ready-to-wear shop and bought a pair of white gloves. His sister bought a pair of panties. In delivery, the packages got mixed up, his sister got the gloves and his sweetheart got the panties. Without examining the contents he sealed the package and sent it to his sweetheart with this note attached:

Dearest Darling;

This little gift is to show you I have not forgotten your birthday. I chose these because I noticed you are not in the habit of wearing any when you go out in the evening. If it had not been for my sister, I would have chosen the long ones with buttons, but she said the short ones are more in fashion and would be easier to remove. These are the delicate shade, but the lady I bought them from showed me the pair she had been wearing for three weeks and they were hardly soiled. I had the sales girl try them on and she really looked sharp.

Now I wish I could put them on for the first time. No doubt other men's hands will come into contact with them before I have a chance to see them again.

When you take them off, blow in them before putting them away, be sure to keep them on while cleaning them or they might shrink. I hope you will like them and wear them on Friday night.

All My love,

P.S. Just think how many times I will kiss the back of them during the coming year. The latest style is to wear them unbuttoned and hanging down.

THERE WAS A MAN WHO REALLY CARED ABOUT HIS BODY. HE LIFTED WEIGHTS, AND JOGGED FIVE MILES EVERY DAY. ONE MORNING HE LOOKED INTO THE MIRROR AND WAS ADMIRING HIS BODY WHEN HE NOTICED THAT HE HAD A BEAUTIFUL TAN ALL OVER EXCEPT FOR HIS PENIS. HE DECIDED TO DO SOMETHING ABOUT IT SO HE WENT TO THE BEACH, COMPLETELY UNDRESSED AND BURIED HIMSELF IN THE SAND EXCEPT FOR HIS PENIS WHICH HE LEFT STICKING OUT.

TWO LITTLE OLD LADIES CAME STROLLING ALONG THE BEACH AND ONE LOOKED DOWN AND SAID "THERE REALLY IS NO JUSTICE IN THIS WORLD". THE OTHER LITTLE OLD LADY ASKED, "WHAT DO YOU MEAN?"

THE FIRST LADY SAID, "LOOK AT THAT!".
"WHEN I WAS 10 YEARS OLD, I WAS AFRAID OF IT,
WHEN I WAS 20 YEARS OLD, I WAS CURIOUS ABOUT IT,
WHEN I WAS 30 YEARS OLD, I ENJOYED IT,
WHEN I WAS 40 YEARS OLD, I ASKED FOR IT,
WHEN I WAS 50 YEARS OLD, I PAID FOR IT,
WHEN I WAS 60 YEARS OLD, I PRAYED FOR IT,
WHEN I WAS 70 YEARS OLD, I FORGOT ABOUT IT,
AND NOW THAT I AM 80, THE DAMNED THINGS ARE GROWING WILD."

Two little boys of grammar school age were to appear in their first play. The first little boy was to say, "Ha, fair maiden, I've come to snatch a kiss and fill your soul with hope." The second little boy was to say, "Hark, a pistol shot."

On the night of the play, the two boys were very nervous, as their parents were in the first row.

The first little boy came out on the stage and said, "Ha, fair lady, I've come to kiss your snatch and fill your hole with soap."

This made the second little boy all the more nervous and he said, "Hark shistol pot, a shostil pit, a postal shit, shit pot, cow shit, bull shit, I didn't want to be in this damn play anyway."

AUTOMATION

A cow is a completely automated milk manufacturing machine. It is encased in untanned leather and mounted on four vertical movable supports, one on each corner. The front end of the machine, or input, contains the cutting and grinding mechanism, utilizing a unique feedback device. Here also are the head-lights, air inlet and exhaust, a bumper, and a foghorn. At the rear, the machine carries the milk-dispensing equipment as well as a built-in flexible fly swatter and insect repeller.

The central portion houses a hydrochemical conversion unit. Briefly, this consists of four fermentation and storage tanks connected in series by an intricate network of flexible plumbing. This part also contains the central heating plant complete with automatic temperature controls, pumping station, and main venti-lating system. The waste disposal apparatus is located to the rear of this central section.

Cows are available, fully assembled, in an assortment of sizes and colors. Production output ranges from two to 20 tons of milk per year. In brief, the main externally visible features of the cow are: two lookers, two hookers, four stander-uppers, four hanger-downers, and a swishy-wishy.

There is a similar machine known as the bull. It gives no milk but has other interesting uses.

THE TWIN BROTHERS

THERE WERE ONCE TWO TWIN BROTHERS, ART, AND JOHN JONES. JOHN WAS MARRIED BUT ART, FOR REASONS UNKNOWN, WAS STILL SINGLE.

THE SINGLE BROTHER, ART, WAS THE OWNER OF A DILAPIDATED ROWBOAT. IT SO HAPPENED THAT JOHN'S WIFE DIED ON THE SAME DAY THAT HIS BROTHER'S ROWBOAT FILLED WITH WATER AND SANK.

A FEW DAYS LATER A KINDLY OLD LADY MET ART ON THE STREET, AND, MISTAKING HIM FOR JOHN, SAID "OH YOU MUST FEEL TERRIBLE."

BUT ART SAID, "I'M NOT SORRY A BIT, SHE WAS A ROTTEN OLD THING FROM THE START. HER BOTTOM WAS ALL CHEWED UP AND SHE SMELLED OF OLD DEAD FISH. THE FIRST TIME I GOT INTO HER, SHE MADE WATER FASTER THAN ANY-THING, AND NO WONDER: SHE HAD A BAD CRACK, AND A PRETTY BAD HOLE IN THE FRONT, AND THE HOLE BEGAN GETTING BIGGER EVERY TIME I USED HER."

"IT GOT SO I COULD HANDLE HER ALL RIGHT, BUT EVERYONE ELSE USING HER SAID SHE LEAKED LIKE NOBODY'S BUSINESS. BUT THIS IS WHAT FINALLY FINISHED HER, FOUR GUYS FROM THE OTHER SIDE OF TOWN WERE LOOKING FOR A GOOD TIME AND ASKED ME IF I WOULD RENT HER TO THEM. WELL, I WARNED THEM THAT SHE WASN'T SO HOT, BUT THEY SAID THEY'D TAKE A CRACK AT HER ANYHOW. ANYWAY, THE CRAZY FOOLS ALL TRIED TO GET INTO HER AT ONCE; IT WAS TOO MUCH FOR HER AND SHE CRACKED RIGHT UP THE MIDDLE.

THE OLD LADY FAINTED DEAD AWAY.

THE ITALIAN WHO WENT TO DETROIT

One-a-day I'ma go to Detroit to a bigga hotel. I go down to eat breakfast. I tella the waitress I wanna two pisses toast. She bring-a-me only one-a-piss. I tella I wanna two piss. She say go to the toilet. I say you no understand. I wanna two piss onna the plate. She say you better no piss onna the plate you sonna-ma-bitch. I don't even know the lady and she calla me a sonna-ma-bitch.

Later I go to eat lunch at a big Restaurant. The waitress bring-a-me a spoon and a knife but no fock. I tella I wanna fock. She tellsa me everybody wanna fock. I tella you no understand. I wanna fock onna the table. She say to-a-me you better no fock onna the table you sonna-ma-bitch.

So, I go back to my room inna hotel and there's no shit onna my bed. I calla the manager and tella him I wanna shit. He tellsa me to go to the toilet, so I say you no understand. I wanna shit onna my bed. He say you better no shit onna the bed you sonna-ma-bitch.

I go check out. The man at the desk he say Peace on you. I say piss onna you too, sonna-ma-bitch.

I go back to ITALY.

SUCH MODESTY!

It seems that a wealthy young playboy out for a night, picked up a beautiful young girl in a bar and took her up to his apartment. Instead of this girl being a tramp, she was well-groomed, chic, and seemingly quite intellectual. Thinking that he would have to impress her to get anywhere, he showed her some etchings, first editions, and finally offered her some wine. He asked whether she would prefer port or sherry.

"Oh, sherry by all means", she said. "Sherry to me is the nectar of the gods. Just looking at it here in its crystal decanter fills me with the anticipation of a heavenly thrill, and when the stopper is removed and this gorgeous liquid is poured into a glass, I inhale the delicious tangy fumes, and I'm lifted on the wings of ecstasy. It seems I taste this magic potion and my whole being seems to glow – a thousand violins throb in my ears and I'm sent into another world." "On the other hand," she said, "Port makes me fart!"

I had 12 bottles Scotch in my house and my wife told me to empty them down the sink 'or else'. So I said I would, and proceeded with the unhappy task.

I withdrew the cork from the first bottle, and poured the contents down the sink with the exception of the one glass which I drank.

I extracted the cork from the second bottle and did likewise with the exception of one glass which I drank.

I withdrew the cork from the third bottle, and emptied the good old booze down the sink, with the exception of one glass which I drank.

I then pulled the cork out of the fourth sink and poured the bottle down the glass, which I drank.
I then pulled the bottle from the cork of the next and drank one sink of it, and drew the rest down the glass.
I pulled the sink out of the next glass, and poured the cork down the next bottle.
I then pulled the next cork from my throat and the sink down the bottle and drank the glass.
Then I corked the sink with the glass, bottled the sink and drank the pour.
When I had everything emptied, I steadied the house with one hand and counted the bottles and corks and glasses with the other which were twenty nine. To be sure I counted them again when they came by, and I had 74, and as the house came by, I counted them again. Finally I had all the houses and bottles and corks and glasses counted except for the one house and the one bottle which I drank.
I am not under the affluence of incohol, as some thinker peep I am, nor am I half so think, as they drunk I am, but I fool so feelish I don't know who is me, and the drunker I stand the longer I get.

The new Priest at his first mass was so nervous he could hardly speak. He asked the old Priest what he should do. The old Priest said he should put a little Gin or Vodka in his water glass before mass, and this would relax him.

The next Sunday, the new Priest filled his water glass with Gin and talked up a storm. After the mass, he asked the old Priest how he did.

The old Priest said "You were relaxed enough, but there are a few things that had to be straightened out:

1. There are Ten Commandments not 12.

2. There are 12 apostles not 10.

3. David slew Goliath, he did not kick the shit out of him.

4. We do not refer to Jesus Christ as the late J.C.

5. And next Sunday there is a Taffy Pulling contest at St Peter's, not a Peter Pulling contest at St Taffy's.

6. And we do not refer to Father, Son, and the Holy Ghost as Big Daddy, Junior, and the Spook."

Whose job is it?

This is a story about four people named Everybody, Somebody, Anybody, and Nobody. There was an important job to be done and Everybody was asked to do it. Everybody was sure Somebody would do it. Anybody could have done it, but Nobody did it. Somebody got angry about that, because it was Everybody's job. Everybody thought Anybody could do it but Nobody realized that Everybody wouldn't do it. It ended up that Everybody blamed Somebody when Nobody did what Anybody could have done.

"INSPIRATION FOR THE UNHAPPY"

Once upon a time there was a little Sparrow who hated
the flight south for the winter. He dreaded the thought
of leaving home so much that he decided to delay the
journey until the last possible minute. After bidding
a fond farewell to all his friends, he went back to his
nest and stayed an additional four weeks. Finally, the
weather turned so bitterly cold that he could delay no
longer. As the Sparrow started south it started to rain,
and in a very short time, ice began to form on his wings.
Almost dead from cold and exhaustion, he fell to earth
in a barnyard. As he was breathing what he thought was
his last breath, a horse walked out of the barn and
covered the little bird with Shit. At first the poor
thing could think of nothing except that this was a
terrible way to die. But as the Shit began to sink into
his feathers, it warmed him and life began to return to
his body. He also found that he had room to breathe.
Suddenly, the little Sparrow was so happy that he started
to sing. At that moment a large cat walked into the
barnyard and hearing the chirping, decided to dig into
the Shit to find out where the sound was coming from.
The cat uncovered the bird and ate it.

THIS STORY HAS THREE MORALS:

1. Not everyone who shits on you is your enemy.

2. Not everyone who takes shit off you is your
    friend.

3. When you are warm and comfortable, even if
    you're in shit up to your eyeballs, keep
    your damn mouth shut!

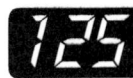

THE
MORNING
MAIL

Dear Earthling,

Hi! I am a creature from outer space. I have transformed myself into this piece of paper. Right now I am having sex with your fingers. I know you like it because you are smiling. Please pass me on to someone else because I'm really horny.

Thanks!

J. S. McMANUS PRODUCE COMPANY

Growers and Shippers of Texas Vegetables

WESLACO, TEXAS 78596

JUNE 4, 1980

TO WHOM IT MAY CONCERN:

THIS IS TO INTRODUCE MRS. GRACIELA GONZALEZ, BETTER KNOWN TO US AS "GOOFY GRACIE". MRS. GONZALEZ HAS BEEN EMPLOYED BY THIS COMPANY FOR A PERIOD OF 4½ YEARS NOT INCLUDING APPROXIMATELY 582 DAYS OFF FOR HANGOVER RECOVERY. HER DUTIES INCLUDE TYPING BILLING ORDERS, LOADING ORDERS, AND TRUCKERS ORDERS, MOST OF THE TIME WITH THE CARBON IN BACKWARDS. SHE DOES A PRETTY GOOD TYPING JOB, OVERLOOKING THE STRIKEOVERS, MISSPELLLED WORDS AND KETCHUP ON THE PAPERS. SHE PREPARES THE PAY-ROLL AND DOES AN EXCELLENT JOB, EXCEPT FOR THE WEEK SHE PAID THE JANITOR $12,672.40. HE IMMEDIATELY CASHED THE CHECK AND DISAPPEARED. GRACIE IS WELL GROOMED, EXCEPT FOR THE OCCASIONAL TIMES SHE SHOWS UP WITH HER JEANS ON INSIDE OUT. SHE IS GOOD-NATURED, AS EVIDENCED BY THE NUMEROUS PROPOSALS SHE RECEIVES FROM THE TRUCKERS.

WE CAN HIGHLY RECOMMEND GRACIE TO ANY COMPANY WHICH DOES NOT FEAR BANKRUPTCY.

SINCERELY YOURS,

BOBBY L. LACKEY
PRESIDENT

BLL/MN

REFERENCES   The First National Bank, Weslaco, Texas   - "Produce Reporter" - "The Packer"

To My Darling Husband:

I am quite aware that you attempted to seduce me 365 times last year (and your score of 12 is probably right) but being a fair and broadminded husband, I am sure you will read and consider some of my complaints also.

To begin with, those excuses I gave you were meant to inspire you, not necessarily stop you. Let's consider my first reason for repulsing you: "We'll wake the children." My - you sure have changed. When we were single and I lived at home, we sometimes did not use the davenport because we were afraid of awakening my parents - but you didn't take "No" for an answer then. You suggested we go for a ride or use pillows on the floor. What's the problem now? We still have a car and pillows. Second reason: "It's too cold." Remember those sub-zero nights in your convertible with cold leather seats - why you even offered to lay your coat on the seat for me, and NOW you accept "too cold or too hot" as excuses.

All the other excuses are only superficial, except the one I believe you really under-rated: "Not in the mood." During our first several years, you'd spend hours and even days just getting me "in the mood" - but now you just pat my "cheeks" and say, "How about a little tonight?" WHAT ELSE DO YOU EXPECT BUT AN EXCUSE? When we were dating, you came to see me all shined up, clean shaven - and you spent money to entertain me. Now we stay at home, you seldom bathe, and expect me to accept love from a cactus bed.

Yes, honey, I thinks we can improve our score this year - if we both spend more time thinking about each other and what we do for each other, rather than what we can get from each other. If you will spend the time it took to prepare your report, and spend that time combing my hair - or bathing with me (like you were doing the night my parents came home early and you had to crawl out of the bathroom window), you will see that I still remember where to hide the soap and hang the wash rag.

Hopefully,

Your loving wife

To my ever loving wife:

During the past year I tried to seduce you 365 times. I succeeded 36 times. This is an average of once every 10 days. For your information I kept a log, and the following is a list of the reasons why I failed.

Reasons:	Times:
We will wake the children	7
It's too late	5
It's too cold	15
It's too hot	23
I'm too tired	52
It's too early	16
Pretending to sleep	49
Window open, neighbors will hear	9
Backache	16
Toothache	4
Giggles	2
Too full	10
Headache	6
Not in the mood	21
Baby crying	10
Watching the late show	7
Watching the early show	5
Mudpack	2
Grease on face	1
Reading the Sunday paper	25
Company in the next room	7
You're too drunk	11
Have to go to the potty	19
Bellyache	7

Do you think you could improve over the coming year?

P.S. And out of the successful times:
    6 times you chewed gum all the while
    5 times you watched T.V. all the time
    18 times you said "Hurry up and get it over with"
    6 times I had to wake you to tell you we were through

And one time I thought I hurt you, because I thought I felt you move.

Your loving, husband,

Dear Friend:

This letter is being sent to you because we know that you are critically interested in your front lawn. This is a fertilizer club and it will not cost you a cent to join.

Upon receipt of this letter go to the first address at the top of the list and shit on the lawn. You will not be the only one there, so don't get embarrassed.

Then make five copies of this letter and send them to five friends who appreciate good lawns. You will not get any money or checks, but within one week if this chain is not broken there will be 9,216 people shitting on your lawn. Your reward will come next summer when you will have the greenest lawn in the neighborhood.

Mrs Harry Butt	Mrs Charles Syringe
236 Corncob Lane	2 Suppository Lane
Mrs Lucy Bowels	Mrs Smelley Behind
29 Bedpan Court	145 Diarrhea Valley
Mrs Opal Crap	Mr G. Howie Farts
1522 Enema Dr.	176 Fertilizer Way
Mr Took A. Physic	Mr A. Big Movement
243 Running Loose Lane	39 Rectum Road

If you are constipated - pass this along to your neighbors. Do not break this chain. One man didn't give a shit and lost his entire lawn!!!!!!

THE RESCUE MISSION
OXFORD ROAD
SWINDON
WILTSHIRE

14 September 1984

Perhaps you have heard of me and my nationwide campaign in the cause of temperance. Each year for the past fourteen, I have made a tour of the British Isles and have delivered a series of lectures on the evils of drink. On this tour, I have been accompanied by my young friend and assistant, Clyde Lindstone.

Clyde - a young man of good family and excellent background - is a pathetic example of a life ruined by excessive indulgence in drink and debauchery. Clyde would appear with me at the lectures and sit on the platform wheezing and swearing at the audience through bleary, bloodshot eyes, sweating profusely, picking his nose, farting and making thoroughly obscene gestures while I would point him out as an example of what evil indulgence can do to a person.

Unfortunately, last autumn, Clyde died.

A mutual friend has given me your name and I wonder if you would be available to take his place on my forthcoming annual tour?

Yours in faith,

The Reverend Elton Jones
THE RESCUE MISSION

17th October, 1961

DOOR - BANGER - STOPPER?

Our door banger stopper has stopped stopping and started banging. If the door banger stopper continues to stop stopping a and carries on banging, the continuous banging of the door banger stopper will result in the banging out of the door stop. We would like the door banger stoppper to stop banging and start stopping.

Will you please attend to this.

R Richardson.
....
Notification Liason Department

LKS/FMH

COPY OF A LETTER FROM A MELBOURNE FARMER IN REPLY TO
AN INCOME TAX FINAL DEMAND

Dear Sirs,

Your letter arrived this morning with a penny stamp on it, my son
and I have gained much pleasure from it, had it not revived in us a
melancholy reflection of what had gone before.

You said the account could have been settled long ago and could
not understand why not, well here is the reason:-

In 1945 I bought a sawmill on credit, in 1955 I bought a team of
horses, two ponies, a timber wagon, a double barrelled shotgun,
and two razor-backed pigs, all on credit. In 1956 the bloody mill
was burnt to the ground, leaving not a damned thing. One of my
ponies died and I loaned the other to a stupid bastard who starved
the poor bugger to death, I then joined the Church.

In 1957 my father died and my brother was hanged for raping a
pensioner. A tramp seduced my daughter and I have to pay the
bastard £50, to prevent him from becoming a relative.

In 1958 my boy had mumps which spread to his balls, and the poor
lad had to be castrated to save his life, later I went fishing and
the rotten boat overturned, sank to the bottom drowning my two
lads, neither being the one who was castrated.

In 1959 my wife ran away with a sheep shearer and he left me with
twins as a souvenir. I employed a house-keeper whom I later
married to keep down expenses. I had a hell of a job trying to
make her pregnant, I saw my doctor who advised me to create some
excitement at the crucial moment. That night, I took my shotgun to
bed with me, at the time I thought was right, I leaned out of the
bed and fired the gun through the window. The result, the wife
shit the bed, I ruptured myself and shot the best cow I ever
owned.

In 1960 someone cut the nuts off my prize bull, I was buggered
completely so I took to drink. I carried on drinking until all I had
left was a pocket watch and one weak bladder. Winding the watch
and running for a piss kept me busy for quite a time. Once
again I took heart. After a year I bought on credit a manure
spreader, a reaper, a binder and a cow. Floods came and washed
the bloody lot away. I was not insured, my wife got V.D. from
a travelling salesman and another son(not the one who was
castrated) wiped his arse on a poisoned rabbit skin and died
from the infection.

You will imagine the surprise on reading that you will cause me
trouble if I do not pay up. If you can think of any trouble I have
missed out on I would very much like to know about it.

Trying to get money out of me is like trying to poke butter up a
porcupine's arse with a red hot needle, I am praying for a shower
of skunk shit to pass over your way and I hope the centre of it
is over the bunch of bastards in your office who sent this final
demand.

> Yours for more credit,
>
> LUCKY LARRY ARKWRIGHT.

SOME GEMS FROM SAVINGS BANK CORRESPONDENCE.

The task of looking after other people's money - and that is what the staffs of our Savings Banks are paid for! - is sometimes lightened by unconscious humour supplied by inconsequential correspondents. We are indebted to Mr H. E. Cotton, Chairman of the Nottingham Publicity Committee, for the following gems from letters received:-

'Just a few lines to say that my book has been mislaid through getting married and being knocked in different places.'

'I beg to inform you that I have married and wish to abide by the rules.'

'Me and my wife desire to dissolve and be made into one, the one being my wife.'

'I beg to inform you that I have changed my address also my wife.!'

'One of our members has fallen out of this book so we are starting a fresh account.'

'I require the money urgently as I am always falling into areas with my landlord.'

'The explanation of the difference of signature was the wife wanting to be too helpful.'

'I drew out three shilling 25 years ago somewhere near Mitcham Railway Bridge. You will find the withdrawal in the corner shop there off the main road.'

'My book was eaten by the dog. I don't see how I can make a special search for it.'

'I have found my book. It was in a piece of music called "God Send You Back To Me".'

'I have no friends or relatives worth mentioning.'

'It seems there is a quarrel as to who shall have my stepfather and his shackels.'

'We have now obtained the execution of our clients.'

'He converted his bonds in 1921 and his wife in 1925.'

'I know the depositor well. It is quite true he has lost his book. He is a very careless man. He has just lost his wife.'

'If you do not receive this, please let me know.'

'I can recall three eights or a couple of threes and eights more or less, but whether this refers to that deposit book or another I do not feel certain.'

'I cannot send my book as requested, as my wife has used it to singe a fowl.'

'Don't forget to add the interest, and make it as much as you can please.'

'The depositor is well known to me. She is my wife.'

IT'S NOT MY FAULT

The ingenuity of drivers involved in accidents in seeking to assert their influence, or at least excuse their errors, is apparently inexhaustible, to judge from this genuine selection of excerpts from insurance claims:

1. I consider that neither vehicle was to blame, but if either were to blame it was the other one.

2. I knocked over a man. He admitted it was his fault as he had been run over before.

3. One wheel went into the ditch, my feet jumped from brake to accelerator pedal, I leaped across to the other side and jammed into the trunk of a tree.

4. I collided with a stationary tram car coming the other way.

5. To avoid collision I ran into the other car.

6. Car had to turn sharper than was necessary owing to an invisible lorry.

7. After the accident a working gentleman offered to be a witness in my favour.

8. I collided with a stationary tree.

9. The other man altered his mind so I had to run over him.

10. I told the other idiot what he was and went on.

11. I can give no details of the accident as I was somewhat concussed at the time.

12. A pedestrian hit me and went under my car.

13. I blew my horn, but it would not work as it was stolen.

14. I unfortunately ran over a pedestrian, and the old gentleman was taken to hospital much regretting the circumstances.

15. I thought the side window was down, but it was up as I found when I put my head through it.

16. Cow wandered into my car. I was afterwards informed that the cow was half-witted.

17. A bull was standing near and a fly must have tickled him as he gored my car.

18. She suddenly saw me, lost her head, and we met.

19. A lorry backed through my windscreen into my wife's face.

20. I ran into a shop window and sustained injuries to my wife.

21. I misjudged a lady crossing the street.

22. Coming home I drove into the wrong house and collided with a tree I haven't got.

23. I left my car unattended for a minute when by accident or design, it ran away.

24. The other car collided with mine without giving any warning of its intentions.

15th December 1977

Dearest John,
  Today the postman brought your sweet gift of Two Turtle Doves. I am delighted, they are adorable. All my love.
                              Your Agnes

16th December 1977

Dear John,
  Oh, how extravagent you really are, I really must protest - I don't deserve such generosity. Three French Hens, I insist you are too kind.
                              Your ever loving Agnes

17th December 1977

Dear John,
  Once again I must protest against such extravagance - Four Calling Birds may be very nice on their own but together with all those other birds they are a bit of a handful.
                              Your Agnes

18th December 1977

Dear John,
  What a surprise. Today the postman delivered Five Golden Rings, one for each finger. You really are an impossible boy but I love you. Frankly all those birds were beginning to squawk and get on my nerves.
                              Your ever loving Agnes.

19th December 1977

Dear John,
  When I opened the door this morning there were actually six bloody great geese laying eggs all over the front step. So, we are back to the birds again. Where on earth do you suppose I can keep them all. The neighbours are beginning to smell them and I can't sleep at night. Please stop.
                              Cordially, Agnes

20th December 1977

John,
  What is it with you and these sodding birds? Now I get Seven Swans a-Swimming. Is it some God-damn joke or what? The house is full of birds, and the racket .....I am beginning to become a nervous wreck. So it is not funny. Stop sending bloody birds.
                              Agnes

21st December 1977

Buster,
  I think I prefer the birds, what the hell am I going to do with Eight Maids a-Milking? It is not enough with all those birds now I have eight cows shitting all over the house and mooing all night. Lay off smartarse.
                              Agnes

22nd December 1977

Dear Joker,
  What are you, some kind of nut? Now I have Nine Pipers Playing and Christ, do they play, when they aren't playing their sodding pipes, they are chasing the maids through the cowmuck. The cows keep mooing and treading all over the bloody birds and the neighbours are threatening to have me evicted.
                              You'll get yours,
                              Agnes

23rd December 1977

Dear rotten bastard,
 Now we have Ten Ladies Dancing! How on earth anyone can call those Ladies, is beyond me. They are all balling the Pipers all night long. The cows can't sleep and have diarrhoea, my living room is a river of manure and the landlords have just declared the building unfit.

                              Piss off,
                                Agnes

24th December 1977

Listen clever bugger,
 What with Eleven Lords-a-leaping-all over the maids, the Ladies and me, we shall never walk again. The Pipers are fighting over the crumpet and are commiting sodomy with the cows, all the birds are dead and rotting amongst the cowmuck. I hope you are satisfied you rotten vicious bastard.

                        Your sworn enemy.
                                Agnes

                 Messrs. Bloggs & Jones. Solicotors.

Dear Sir,
 This is to acknowledge your gift of Twelve Fiddlers Fiddling with themselves. We understand this is the latest infliction on our client, Miss Agnes Fullbody, who now resides at the Happy Hours Sanitorium. We are asked to charge you with total destruction of our client's home, sanity and genital's. Please do not attempt to contact Miss Fullbody who has given instructions to the staff to have you shot on sight. Please find enclosed a Warrant for your arrest.

                        Yours faithfully.

                        Bloggs & Jones.

ONE FOR THE WALL

This is

NATIONAL

WEEK

If you gave at the
OFFICE

YOU NEED NOT GIVE
AT HOME!

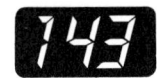

YOUR
MOTHER
DOESN'T WORK HERE!
YOU WILL HAVE TO PICK UP
AFTER YOURSELF!!!!!

When you are up to your ass
in alligators, it is difficult to
remind yourself that
your initial objective was
to drain the swamp.

PEOPLE WHO THINK THEY KNOW EVERYTHING ARE PARTICULARLY AGGRAVATING TO THOSE OF US WHO DO.

NOTICE

THIS PLACE REQUIRES NO PHYSICAL FITNESS PROGRAM.

EVERYONE GETS ENOUGH EXERCISE,

JUMPING TO CONCLUSIONS,

FLYING OFF THE HANDLE,

RUNNING DOWN THE BOSS,

KNIFING FRIENDS IN THE BACK,

DODGING RESPONSIBILITY

AND

PUSHING THEIR LUCK!

"Bad Planning on Your Part Does Not Necessarily Constitute an Automatic Emergency on My Part"

R. I. P.

If you work and do your best,
    You'll get the sack like all the rest,

But if you laze, and muck about,
    You'll live to see the job right out,

The work is hard, the pay is small,
    So take your time, and sod 'em all,

'Cause when your dead, you'll be forgot,
    So don't try to do, the bleeding lot,

Or on your tombstone neatly lacquered,
    Will be three words.

"JUST BLOODY KNACKERED"

LABOUR RATE

AT THIS GARAGE IS AS FOLLOWS

	PER HOUR
MINIMUM RATE	£ 3.50
CUSTOMERS WATCHING	£ 4.50
CUSTOMERS GIVING ADVICE	£ 6.00
CUSTOMERS HELPING	£ 10.00

MAKE
SOMEONE
HAPPY

"stop using the
Bloody Phone!"

"Yea, though I walk
through the valley
of the shadow of death
I shall fear no evil.
Cause I am the meanest
"Son of a Bitch
in the valley."

**"Patience, my ass!
I'm gonna kill something!"**

Deadline? Nobody told me anything about a fucking deadline.